Illustrated Guide to

FLOWERING TOBACCO

for

GARDENS

RICHARD POCKER

ISBN: 1500800856
ISBN 13: 9781500800857
Library of Congress Control Number: 2014914395
CreateSpace Independent Publishing Platform
North Charleston, South Carolina

Dedicated to Audrey Pocker
1924–2011

A Perfect Gardener

TABLE OF CONTENTS

INTRODUCTION

Their beauty is appealing, and their fragrance is alluring. Nicotiana (ni-co-she-AA-nah), or flowering tobacco, is a lovely heirloom flower gaining recognition among today's gardeners. This ornamental fills the summer garden with large, brightly colored trumpets of star-shaped flowers that attract butterflies and hummingbirds. Older nicotiana species are valued for their impressive stature and deliciously scented flowers that open in early evening. Newer hybrids offer smaller, more compact plants with abundant flowers that bloom throughout the summer.

Source: National Garden Bureau

During a road trip in the summer of 1999, I stumbled upon a county fair in North Carolina. I was mesmerized by some of the exhibits. As a born and bred Yankee, I was astonished by the politically incorrect exhibits for tobacco farming—tobacco seeds, co-op assistance, services for disease control, and increasing crop yield.

Bumper stickers with quotes such as "Tobacco Paid for This Vehicle" abounded. In an age where the words "smoking" and "cancer" were always spoken in the same sentence, these displays were unfathomable.

However, I retained a residual contrarian streak from my younger years. I am also a hobbyist gardener with a love of practicing hands-on American history, so I decided to try my green thumb growing this plant that had so much influence on the history of America and the world. It frequently happens to me that my hobbies get out of hand. At the end of one summer, my garden was awash in seven hundred plants.

The flowers attracted an amazing numbers of hummingbirds and butterflies. The lime-green, bell-shaped flowers of the Langsdorfii nicotiana were captivating. The sweet-smelling Jasmine flooded the field at night with scent. The long, tubular blossom of the Sylvestris variety was a magnet for butterflies. The reddish-pink flowers of the Havana varieties were irresistible to hummingbirds.

Obtaining a nursery license for New York State, I began to sell seedlings at the local farmers market. Scores of converts began to plant this incredible variety of attractor. Exhibiting at a local agricultural show, strangely with little competition, over time the plants began to win ribbons. In 2007, I won the blue ribbon (with the ten-dollar prize money) for best in show for Miscellaneous Field Crops.

Every year I searched for new varieties of nicotiana. Some of them I was able to easily germinate and grow successfully. Others required more experimentation to find the right mix of soil, sunlight, and care. This book is a summary of my experience. It can never be complete, as I am still learning every year.

This illustrated guide is for the gardener who wants to grow something out of the ordinary. Nicotiana not only becomes a visual focus on your garden, but also a talking point, a conversation piece, if you will. My emphasis is on the beauty of the flower and the plant rather than its uses.

Some varieties can grow up to eight feet tall with leaves almost three feet long. There are nicotiana flowers that will to fill the garden with incredible perfume. Others are nursery hybrids that grow no more than a foot tall. Within the hundreds of types of nicotiana, heirloom, native, nursery hybrids, and commercial hybrids, there is something for every garden. This volume covers nicotiana commonly available—heirloom, native, and nursery hybrids.

The purpose of this guide is to illustrate the use of nicotiana as an ornamental plant for the garden and to relate some history of the plant.

It is generally agreed to by thinking adults that tobacco usage may lead to cancer. This is NOT a guide for the use of tobacco leaves or preparing them for smoking or chewing.

Because I am writing this for my fellow hobbyist gardener, common names for the varieties are used. There may be some confusion as the same common name may be used for several varieties. I have done my best to clarify where those overlaps occur.

In addition to the photos, descriptions of the flowers and the leaves are emphasized. Most of these varieties are excellent container plants, both indoors and out. Their growth will be restricted by the space for their roots, and they will change size accordingly. As for zone hardiness, I can only depend upon my own experience to say that I have grown many of these in Nova Scotia with the short but intense growing season. Ninety percent of the world's tobacco grows in the temperate zone between forty degrees north and south, but it can be successfully raised as far north as Alaska and Greenland and as far south as New Zealand.

The listed sources for seeds are as current as possible and include instructions for growing tobacco from seed and the care of plants. Some seeds are rare, and sources may be out of stock during one season. Keep searching online. Part of the fun of growing heirloom tobaccos is the excitement of the hunt and making new friends along the way.

There is a chapter about how to save the seeds. Seed exchanges can be found online, and trades are a method of enlarging your collection.

There are new hybrid nursery varieties that are smaller and fit into compact garden beds or containers. The selection of available varieties is constantly expanding. Started bedder plants may be found at local nurseries. Nicotiana is beginning to be discovered as an interesting ornamental that has a place in the garden.

I have relied on extensive research for sources and my own experience in writing this book. Any errors are my own, and I invite and would appreciate the reader's input for corrections or suggestions to future editions. E-mail me at richard@floweringtobacco.com

I have enjoyed more than a decade of seed hunting, growing, photographing, and exhibiting nicotiana plants. I have made friends around the world that share my interest in the plant, for its beauty and its effects on history. It is time for you to discover this underused and underappreciated versatile plant.

Richard Pocker
Millbrook, NY

Chapter 1

IN THE GARDEN AND THE HOUSE

Nicotiana is a much-underutilized variety of plant that can bring a garden to a new level of interest and excitement. Plants grouped together or strategically placed about, tobacco has some of the most unique blossoms and foliage.

The most popular heirloom nicotiana, Sylvestris, has thick, green stems with pale leaves and clusters of long, tubular, white trumpet flowers. Another favorite is Langsdorfii. It has tall, sturdy stems and two-inch long, apple green, drooping flowers. Jasmine is the most fragrant of all the nicotiana. Be sure to plant some near a window, either in the ground or planters, to have the nighttime fragrance waft into your home.

Never one to do anything in half measures, early in my discovery of flowering tobacco, I attempted to grow more than fifty varieties one year.

I was awash in more than seven hundred plants, but I still call it my "summer of butterflies." My garden was overwhelmed. It was also an extraordinary hummingbird attractor.

Photo: Richard Pocker © **Different Varieties of Heirloom Tobacco**

Whether you tend to garden in moderation or with abandon, nicotiana is very easy to grow, and the results are breathtaking.

Photo: Richard Pocker © **Havana 608 in Vegetable Garden (upper left).**
The flowers will attract butterflies and bees, but that section of ground is
unusable as a food plot for many years.

Tobacco plants add interest to a vegetable garden. It will attract butterflies, bees, and hummingbirds. **Once used for tobacco, do not plan to use the ground as a food plot in the future. Tobacco is toxic. Please use common sense.**

There are a dozen special varieties of hybrid nicotiana bred for gardens. Ranging in many colors and blooms, they are easy to maintain, and their compact size allows a wider range of design. Saratoga, Starmaker, and Domino are often found at nurseries for gardeners who prefer to plant bedder stock.

Photo: Dobies, UK © **Domino Mixed in the Garden**

Many nicotiana varieties make excellent cut flowers.

Tobacco plants can be miniaturized, much like bonsai. Follow the instructions in the chapter STARTING SEEDS. Once the plants have outgrown their starting tray, it is time to transplant them to a larger container. Trim away the bottom third of the roots before transplanting. It will not damage the plant, and it will restrict the growth. The plants need light, so if you do not have a south-facing window, compact florescent light will work.

They need to be kept well watered, and after three to four weeks, they need to be fertilized once a week.

Chapter 2

STARTING NICOTIANA PLANTS FROM SEEDS

With dozens of heirloom varieties to choose from, the seed selection can seem overwhelming. Many seeds are easy to start, while others require patience. Be prepared to experiment. The suppliers for seeds are listed on each descriptive page as well as in the "Source" section of this book.

Nicotiana seeds are tiny. A teaspoon is enough to plant an acre. Seeds from mail-order suppliers will come in small packets of about fifty to one hundred seeds.

Photo: Richard Pocker ©

A teaspoon of seeds is enough to plant an acre of tobacco

To start the seeds indoors, any dome-type, seed-starting tray is sufficient. Start them about four to eight weeks before the last frost. It is best to keep one variety per tray. You can also use pots or trays filled with a seed-starting mix that is filled almost to the top.

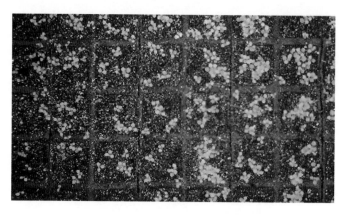

Photo: Richard Pocker © **Two weeks**

To start the seeds directly in the soil outdoors, once the soil is warm, mixing the seeds with fine sand will help control the even spread and help retain some moisture and hold them in place.

In the cells or trays, the seeds are lightly pressed on top of the soil. Do not cover them with soil. Nicotiana seeds need light to germinate. Only two to three seeds per cell are needed. Some seeds will germinate faster than others will. Keep the cells moist. A mister or watering from below is best.

Place the trays in a warm location until they begin to germinate. They can be moved to a sunny location or under plant lights as soon as they begin to geminate.

You should be able to trim back to the strongest plant in a cell by cutting back the weakest ones when they are at the stage of developing two leaves. If too many seeds sprout on a cell, you will be able to soak and separate the plants later, but it is best to be sparing with the seeds when sowing them. They will reach transplanting size in about six to seven weeks.

Photo: Richard Pocker © **Transplanted seedlings about seven weeks**

Nicotiana must be hardened off, as the seedlings are very sensitive to light and temperature. After six weeks or so, when they reach about three inches in height, on the first warm day, take the trays outside and put them in the shade. Bring them back in at night for a few days.

This hardening off is essential. It was the reason for my crop failures for the first few attempts I made at raising tobacco. In the Northeast, once you miss the critical window for starting the seed, there is no second chance. If you live in an area with more than one growing season, it is not as disastrous if you lose the first crop.

After they have been hardened off, if necessary, soak the soil in the cell and separate them for transplanting. Transplant them into pots or directly into your garden when the temperatures are warm enough.

Using pots may control the height of the plants. If you choose to plant directly in the ground, remember that nicotiana is toxic. **DO NOT MIX TOBACCO AND FOOD PLANTS TOGETHER.**

Photo: Richard Pocker © **Tobacco plants at 12 weeks**

Chapter 3

CLASSIFICATION AND VARIETIES

Nicotiana is a member of the Solanaceae or Nightshade family. Its closest flower relative is the petunia, and it is also related to tomatoes, peppers, eggplants, and potatoes. The heirloom species that are featured in this volume are native to tropical South America, primarily Argentina and Brazil.

Heirloom tobaccos generally reach five feet or more in height. The hybrid garden varieties have been bred to stay much smaller, twelve to eighteen inches. Their range of colors and compactness makes them more versatile in the smaller garden, but they lack the dramatic effects of large leaves and unusual flowers.

What Are Heirlooms & Hybrids

These old-fashioned types of tobacco, commonly referred to as heirloom, have been around for many decades and carry with them some interesting names we know little about...They are pure in a sense that their genetic characteristics have not been modified over time through cross-pollination with other types. As a true breed, if you were to grow one hundred plants, there would be little difference between one and another. Also, were you to collect the seeds from one of these and grow them the following year, you'd get very similar results.

By contrast, there are also a mind-boggling number of hybrids, which often have coded names. These varieties have been produced by crossbreeding one type of tobacco with another to produce a new variety. It's what modern-day tobacco farmers grow. Hybrids pertain to contain the most favorable characteristics of tobacco, while keeping out unwanted features.

If you were to grow one hundred hybrid tobacco plants, there would, as with heirlooms, be little difference between one and another. However, were you to collect the seeds from one of these and grow them the following year, there would be little similarity between them. The seeds will produce plants resembling one or the other parent or both, but there will be considerable variations between them.

So with heirloom seeds, you buy these once and can grow them forever after. Hybrids are grown once, and each year you need to buy fresh seeds to avoid them turning back into their more primitive state.

There are benefits and drawbacks associated with each type.

In the end, it boils down to personal taste and one's point of view. Heirloom types are more traditional and can be resown as many times as you please, whereas hybrids are the result of applied science and some prefer the more interesting flavors, but seeds must be bought again, every year.
The Tobacco Seed Company website

Types of Heirloom Tobaccos

There are classifications for most varieties of heirloom tobaccos that relate to their method of being cured for use of the leaves. Although this book is not covering that topic, there is no escaping the nomenclature, as the terms that are associated with the type will crop up time and time again. Briefly, this is an explanation of the terms of the principle types:

Fire-Cured
Hung over gently smoking fires, it is a very robust type used in pipes and chewing tobacco.

Brightleaf
Also known as "Virginia Tobacco," no matter where in the world it is grown. It was developed in the early nineteenth century. The

process was developed by a slave who accidentally discovered the process of using a heated stove to cure the leaf. Able to grow in poor, sandy soil, brightleaf dominated the tobacco market in the South, and during the Civil War, Northern soldiers passing through brought the habit home with them, developing a national market.

Burley

Discovered in Ohio, the market developed after the Civil War. It cures to a very light yellow to white in color. It soon spread to Kentucky and Tennessee and is the variety most people associate with tobacco.

Oriental

Highly aromatic and grown primarily in Greece, Lebanon, and Turkey, this type is also known as Persian tobacco. The leaves are small and, because of its strong flavor, are used in blending with lighter tobaccos.

Perique

Found only in Saint James Parish in Louisiana, it is the strongest flavored of all the tobaccos. Used as a blending tobacco for pipes, it is the only tobacco cured by pressure and fermentation.

Shade

Primarily grown in Connecticut and Massachusetts, it is grown under large tents to protect the leaf from direct sunlight. Prized as a cigar wrapper, the process of harvesting is very labor intensive. It remains the only tobacco exported to Cuba to wrap their cigars prior to the embargo.

Rustica

Found in the wild, it was used by natives from the United States, Mexico, and South America. Australia has several varieties still used by the Aboriginal people.

Nomenclature

Ornamental types of nicotiana are commonly called flowering to-bacco, leading to some confusion since there are many variations in size, color, and fragrance between the species and hybrids. Older heirloom species are often identified by their genus and species name. Its genus name, designated by Linnaeus in 1753, recognizes Frenchman Jean Nicot, ambassador to Portugal from 1559–1561, who brought powdered tobacco to France to cure the queen's son of migraine headaches. Many of the species names refer to a characteristic of the plant. Nicotiana alata gets its species name from the Latin alata, meaning winged, for the winged petioles of the leaves. N. sylvestris, from the Latin sylva, meaning of the forest or woodland possibly refers to its native habitat. N. langsdorffii was named after G. I. Langsdorf, the Russian Consul in Rio de Janeiro who organized an expedition to explore the inner regions of Brazil in the 1820s.

National Garden Bureau

It is fairly easy to identify the type of nicotiana when it carries several names. For example, nicotiana sylvestris is found under the common names of South American tobacco, Argentine tobacco, Indian Peace Pipe tobacco, Flowering, Only the Lonely, White Tobacco, and Woodland tobacco, among a few others.

The confusion begins when the same common name is shared by several different varieties. The name "Desert Tobacco" is shared by both nicotiana obtusifolia and nicotiana trigonophylla. Indian tobacco is shared among several varieties. There are notations with the descriptions of each variety to clarify this problem when it occurs.

Appendix C is an index of common names of the varieties featured in this book with synonyms. Keep in mind, there is still widespread disagreement among the experts regarding the names of the cultivars.

To understand the complexity of name identifications in botanical research, visit www.theplantlist.org, use the search term "nicotiana," and work with the interactive features related to the naming nicotiana varieties.

Appendix D is an extensive list of heirloom, nursery hybrid, and commercial hybrid types. They are culled from years of searching. Some have been unavailable for decades, but they are included for those who are interested in further botanical, horticultural, or historical research.

Chapter 4

HEIRLOOM TOBACCO

I have enjoyed raising heirloom nicotiana, both for the plant and the flower. Heirlooms have an extensive variety in appearance, and the historical connections are fascinating.

The list of sources is as current as possible, but you may find that as fashion or demand dictates, new varieties are available and others have disappeared. It is part of the fun of seed hunting to track them down.

Seed traders can also be found on online auction sites such as eBay. There are seed exchanges online that also have nicotiana for sale or trade.

ACUMINATA

Photo: Daggawalla Seeds © **Acuminata tobacco**

Common Names: Many Flower Tobacco; Tabaco Silvestre; Tabaco de Cerro; Wild Tobacco

Binominal Name: Nicotiana tabacum acuminata

Acuminata is a native tobacco of Chile. It is found in arid areas from the coast to as high as the tree line. It thrives in poor, sandy soil and is ideal for rock gardens. Hardier than the other native Chilean tobacco, Cimarron, Acuminata is able to withstand colder temperature and is recommended to USDA Zone 8. It is also found in the wild in California as an invasive plant. It grows to about 36–38 inches with blade-shaped leaves. It requires full sun. Space the plants 16–20 inches apart.

It has many five-pointed, pure-white flowers, and the ends of branching stems have a faint scent of tomatoes. As a fellow member of the Solanaceae family, perhaps the tomato scent should not be too surprising. It is an unusual addition to your garden. The seeds are rare and may require some searching when these sources are out of stock.

Sources:
Daggawalla
Chileflora.com

AFFINIS

Photo: Cibergarden.com © **Affinis Tobacco Flower**

Common Names: Affinis; Alata Persian Tobacco

Binominal Name: Nicotiana tobacaum affinis

This is one of the more confusing nomenclatures of nicotiana. Persian tobaccos are sweet scented and crossbred with several other varieties both to enhance the scent and to bring more color to the flowers.

Jasmine, (see **Jasmine**) one of the most popular because of its strong evening scent, is a variety of affinis crossed with grandiflora. Lime Green is another variety of affinis. Many suppliers of seeds have created their own names and specifications.

What they all share in common is a charming, star-shaped flower waving on a thin stalk and with various degrees of a delicious, sweet scent. They grow 36 to 48 inches high with full sun but will tolerate partial shade. Space the plants 12–16 inches apart in well-drained soil. The flowers last all summer. However, when ordering seeds, check the description carefully for the color you want. Under the label of affinis, you will find everything from purple to pure white.

Photo: Cibergarden.com © **Affinis Plant**

Sources:
Cibergarden, Spain
Chiltern, UK
Dobies, UK
Northwood Seeds
Nuts n Cones, UK
Plant World Seeds, UK
Richbar
Victory Seeds
White Flower Farms (plants only)
Suttons Seeds, UK
Virginia Tobacco SeIain

AFRICAN RED

Photo: northwoodseeds.com. © **African Red Tobacco**

Common Name: African Red

Binominal Name: Nicotiana tabacum african red

This is a large-leaf variety that can reach over 8 feet in height. It has a sturdy stalk with leaves that are about 24 inches long and 12 inches wide. They are a light-green color with white stems. This nicotiana does best in full sun. Space the plants 16–20 inches apart in loose, well-drained loam.

The unusually tight, columnar-shaped plant is topped with clusters of pink/red flowers.

It matures in eight days, and the leaves turn dark-red when cured.

The original seeds came from Transvaal, South Africa.
Sources:

Northwood Seeds
The Tobacco Seed Co., UK
Sustainable Seeds

BAFRA

Photo: Daggawalla Seeds © **Bafra Tobacco Flower**

Common Names: Bafra; Bafra Turkish

Binominal Name: Nicotiana tabacum bafra

Bafra is a city on the Black Sea in the Turkish tobacco-growing province of Samsun. An Oriental heirloom tobacco, Bafra is raised for its particular flavor not for leaf yield, hence the smaller leaves than those normally found on nicotiana tabacum. This plant has a columnar shape with heart-shaped, velvet-textured leaves. Bafra grows to 150 cm (60 in) and is topped with clusters of white flowers tinged in pink. It is an exceptional hummingbird attractor.

Photo: Daggawalla Seeds **Bafra Tobacco**

Sources:
Daggawalla
Northwood
New Hope
The Seed Store
Sustainable Seeds

BAIANO

*Photo: Daggawalla Seeds © **Baiano Tobacco***

Common Names: Baiano; Baiano Hungarian

Binominal Name: Nicotiana tabacum baiano

Hungarian-type tobaccos were bred in Eastern Europe in the Austro-Hungarian Empire. They tend to be stronger in flavor and are therefore classified as an Oriental tobacco, which is blended in small amounts with other types of tobacco to add flavor. It grows to about 36 to 48 inches high. Space the plants 18–24 inches apart in loose, well-drained soil. The leaves of Baiano are thick and heavy with a velvet texture. The column of leaves folds up at night. This allows Baiano to tolerate moderate frosts. The flowers are densely packed pink, which attracts hummingbirds.

Sources:
Daggawalla Seeds
Northwood Seeds
Virginia Tobacco Seeds, Spain
Sustainable Seeds

BANANA LEAF

Photo: northwoodseeds.com **Banana Leaf Tobacco Flower**

Common Name: Banana Leaf

Binominal Name: Nicotiana tabacum banana leaf

Banana Leaf is an heirloom variety, brightleaf or "Virginia" to-bacco. Brightleaf tobaccos tend to turn yellow as they ripen, and leaves are harvested from the bottom up as this happens. The clus-ters of trumpet-shaped flowers are white, tinged with pink. These varieties are raised for their light flavor and yield. They grow to 72 inches or more. The leaves on this plant are long and narrow, about 30 inches long and 12 inches wide. Full sun is required for the best growth, but they have a tolerance for a wide range of soils. They are excellent butterfly and hummingbird attractors.

Photo: northwoodseeds.com **Banana Leaf Tobacco**

Sources:
New Hope
The Tobacco Seed Co., UK
Virginia Tobacco Seeds, Spain
West Seed Farm
Northwood Seeds
Sustainable Seeds

BARINAS

Photo: Beth B. Pocker © **Barinas Tobacco Flower**

Common Name: Barinas

Binominal Name: Nicotiana tabacum barinas

Barinas is one of the oldest cultivated varieties of tobacco. Discovered growing in the Barinas area of Venezuela, the Spanish began to ship it back to Europe in the early 1500s. It is rumored that Venetian traders introduced it to Eastern Europe where strains of it became the basis of most Turkish style tobaccos. The Dutch, raiding the Spanish Main and by way of Curacao, introduced it to Europe as well.

With clusters of pink flowers and a thick stalk, Barinas is a hummingbird and butterfly attractor. It is a very rare variety, and the seeds are often unavailable but worthwhile to track it down.
The leaves are small but heavy and supported by a thick stalk. They are spaced apart, 15 to 18 inches long and 9 inches wide.

Plants need full sun. Space them 16–20 inches apart in loose, well-drained loam.

Photo: Richard Pocker © **Barinas Tobacco**

Sources:
Heirloom Tobacco
The Tobacco Seed Co., UK
Sustainable Seeds

BASMA

Photo: Cibergarden © **Basma Tobacco**

Common Names: Basma; Black Sea Basma; Turkish Basma

Binominal name: Nicotiana tabacum basma

Grown exclusively in western Greece, Basma is a low nicotine content nicotiana that is raised for its strong flavor as a blending agent. The stalks are sturdy but flexible. The plants are shorter than usual nicotiana, and the oval leaves are small. The leaves turn yellow to light red when cured. It has clusters of pink flowers. It thrives in dry climates and is also suitable as an indoor plant. Space the plants 12–16 inches apart. It is slow growing, so be patient if comparing its growth to other nicotiana in your garden.

Again, a rare variety so some searching may be necessary.

Sources:
Cibergarden, Spain
Sustainable Seeds
Tobacco Seed Co., UK
Virginia Tobacco Seeds, Spain

BIG GEM

Photo: northwoodseeds.com © **Big Gem Tobacco**

Common Name: Big Gem

Binominal Name: Nicotiana tabacum big gem

Big Gem is an heirloom brightleaf variety with leaves that grow to 36 inches long and 18 inches wide. Leaves grow on alternating sides of the sturdy stalk and fill in big spaces. Clusters of pink flowers (the plant in the photo has been topped off to promote leaf growth). This is a fast-growing giant that matures in forty-four to sixty days. Plant them in full sun with loose, well-drained soil.

Sources:
Northwood Seeds
The Tobacco Seed Company
New Hope Seeds
Sustainable Seeds

BIGELOVII

Photo: Daggawalla Seeds © **Bigelovii Tobacco**

Common Names: Bigelovii; Big Love; Indian Tobacco

Binominal Name: Nicotiana tabacum bigelovii

Native to California, it is found in nature in the western Mojave Desert. Easily recognized by its large, showy white flowers. The flower tube is almost 5 cm (2 in) long ending in a bloom of bright white.

Like most wild tobacco, the stalks are thin and branching, the leaves are small and narrow, and the attention is on the flower. The plant grows to about 24 to 36 inches high. It thrives in semiarid climates in poor soil. The seeds are rare and might require some searching, but they are worth the effort.

Source:
Daggawalla
Allies

BLACK SEA SAMSUN

Photo: Daggawalla Seeds © **Black Sea Samsun Tobacco**

Common Names: Black Sea Samsun; Samsun Tobacco

Binominal Name: Nicotiana tabacum black sea samsun

Originated and grown in the Black Sea region of Turkey, this heirloom variety is raised for its rich aroma and flavor. It has heart-shaped leaves with clusters of pink/purplish flowers. It grows to 36 to 48 inches high in loose loam to sandy soil but needs full sun for best growth. Space the plants 12–16 inches apart. The leaves have a distinctive aroma in the garden. It is a wonderful container plant.

Sources:
Daggawalla
Northwood Seeds
The Tobacco Seed Co., UK
Cibergarden, Spain
Sustainable Seeds
New Hope
Victory Seeds
Virginia Tobacco Seeds, Spain
West Seed Farm
Brown Leaf

BROWN LEAF

Photo: Richard Pocker © **Brown Leaf Tobacco**

Common Names: Brown Leaf; Virginia Brown Leaf

Binominal Name: Nicotiana tabacum brown leaf

Primarily grown for its large and light leaves that grow up to 36 inches long. Although classified as a Virginia-type tobacco, the leaves cure to a dark brown rather than light, golden yellow, as others in that classification. The plant is topped with a cluster of pink flowers that, like other Virginia and burley-type tobaccos, is a hummingbird and butterfly attractor.

Plant them in a loose, well-drained loam and water frequently. Full sun is needed for the best growth. Space them 20–24 inches apart.

Sources:
B&T
JL Hudson
Rostliny-Semena—Czech
Burley Heirlooms

BURLEY HEIRLOOMS

Photo: Richard Pocker © **Burley Tobacco Flower**

Common Names: Burley; Burley 21; Burley 64; Gold Dollar; Golden Burley; Green Brior; Harrow Velvet; KY 5; KY14; KY17; KY21; KY 907; Monte Calme Blonde; Monte Calme Yellow; TN 86; TN 90; TND 950; Virginia 509; Warner, Yellow Twist Bud

First discovered on a farm in Ohio in 1865, the light-shaded leaf of air-cured burley was a commercial success. Burley tobacco encompasses dozens of variations. They share a common trait of being a light, air-cured tobacco that is primarily used in cigarette production. Today, 10 percent of world production of tobacco is burley.

With thick and sturdy stalks, the leaves grow 24 to 36 inches long and 12 to 24 inches wide. The leaves turn to a golden yellow at the end of the season. The leaves begin to yellow at the bottom of the stalk.

Burleys tolerate a wide range of soils from loose loam to limestone. The flowers grow in dense clusters and range in color from a pink to rosy red. They are excellent butterfly and humming-bird attractors. Seventy percent of burley tobacco is grown in Kentucky.

The photo below shows the beginning of the ripening of burley on the stalk.

Photo: Richard Pocker ©

Burley KY 907 begins to ripen from the bottom leaves upward

Because burleys are primarily propagated for commercial grow-ers, they are large plants. Planting them in containers can control plant size, or try to Bonzai them. They are fun to experiment with. Shop around and try a selection.

Most burleys are similar in appearance for our purposes as ornamentals in the garden, and their differences are primarily in the dried-leaf coloring, uses, and flavor as harvested tobacco, and disease resistance (more about that in the chapter DISEASES), which is of importance to commercial farmers but in most cases of secondary interest to the gardener.

This source list is of suppliers of seeds that are readily available in small quantities. In the APPENDIX is a comprehensive list of both heirloom and commercial varieties. Some commercial varieties are no longer available but included for those readers who are interested in botanical or historical research.

Sources:
Burley:
Chiltern, UK
The Tobacco Seed Co., UK

Burley 21:
Sustainable Seeds
Northwood Seeds

Burley 64:
Northwood Seeds

Burley-Deutschland:
Virginia Tobacco Seeds, Spain

Burley-Gold Dollar:
New Hope; Northwood Seeds
The Tobacco Seed Co., UK
Sustainable Seeds

Burley-Golden Burley:
New Hope
Northwood Seeds
Sustainable Seeds
The Tobacco Seed Co., UK
Victory Seeds

Burley-Green Brior:
New Hope
Northwood Seeds
Sustainable Seeds
West Seed Farm

Burley-Harrow Velvet:
New Hope
Northwood Seeds
Sustainable Seeds
The Tobacco Seed Co., UK
Virginia Tobacco Seeds, Spain

Burley-KY14:
JL Hudson

Burley-KY 15:
Sustainable Seeds

Burley-KY 17:
B&T; JL Hudson
Sustainable Seeds

Burley-KY21:
West Seed Farm
New Hope

Burley-KY 5:
West Seed Farm
New Hope
Burley-KY 907:
JL Hudson

Burley-KY 190:
Sustainable Seeds

Burley-KY 8635:
Sustainable Seeds

Burley-Monte Calme Yellow:
The Tobacco Seed Co., UK
B&T
Northwood Seeds

Burley-TN 86:
JL Hudson
Northwood Seeds
Victory Seeds

Burley-TN 86 LC:
Sustainable Seeds
Northwood Seeds

Burley-TN 90:
B&T
JL Hudson
Cibergarden, Spain
Northwood Seeds
Virginia Tobacco Seeds, Spain

Burley-TN 90 LC:
Northwood Seeds
Sustainable Seeds

Burley-TND 950:
JL Hudson

Burley-Virginia 509:
JL Hudson
Northwood Seeds
Sustainable Seeds

Burley-Yellow Twist Bud:
New Hope
Northwood Seeds
Victory Seeds
Sustainable Seeds
West Seed Farm

By the time Thomas Jefferson was born in Albemarle County in 1743, Virginia had been awash in tobacco since the early 1620s. In almost every nook and cranny, tobacco was grown, often to the neglect of food production. The reason was simple; it meant cash to the colonist, who despite their hardy pedigrees often preferred a life of leisure to hard work.

In the early 17[h] century when the original royal charters for the Virginia colonies were granted by James I and Charles I., tobacco was not among the commodities in demand in England.

Colonies were wildly expensive to finance and maintain. In exchange, the kings expected them to provide the mother country with goods such as furs, hemp, wine, fruit, salt, potash, tar, pitch, and fish. England, being resource poor, was forced to pay high prices for these commodities from Spain, Holland Portugal, and France. It also left her vulnerable in times of war when these resources would be cut off.

However, colonists found tobacco farming more suited to their temperament than the backbreaking labors of mining or trapping. It would take many generations for things to smooth out and for England to receive a greater variety of raw materials she so desperately needed.

The colonial planter, sending his hogsheads of tobacco to a British merchant in London on consignment, waited months or years for payment. In the interim, the farmer would borrow money from another London agent, called a Factor, against the expected amount due. Accepting credit against goods ordered from London, the farmer later had to accept whatever amount of money the agent offered to pay. This amount was usually far less than the credit extended by the Factor, and a never-ending cycle of crushing debt was begun.

Jefferson, whose own debts were eventually paid off by his grandchildren, wrote:

*These debts had become hereditary from father to son so that plant-
ers were a species of property, annexed to certain mercantile houses
in London.*

In another letter, he noted:

*No other law can be more oppressive to the mind or fortune, and
long experience has proven to us there was never an instance of a
man's getting out of debt who was in the hands of a tobacco merchant & bound to consign his tobacco to him. It is the most abusive
of all snares.*

Although Jefferson never shied from his financial obligations, not all of
the Virginia planting class held his high-minded ideals. Many hoped that
a break from England would be the end of their debts. By 1776, Virginias
owed English merchants over £2,000,000. The amount was more than all
the other colonies combined.

Englishmen to the core and reluctant to join the revolutionary New
Englanders, the prospect of debt relief tipped the scales in supporting the
break with the king of England.

Imagine their chagrin when the Treaty of Paris was signed in 1786, se-
curing America's place as an independent nation and ending the War of
Rebellion. One of the main provisos of the treaty clearly allowed London
merchants to continue their efforts to collect money owed them, causing
William Randolph, one of Virginia's largest landholders, to cry out in an-
guish: "What did we fight this war for?"

BURLEY TOBACCO COMMERCIAL HYBRIDS

Photo: Colonies Project.com © **A Field of Ripening Burley Tobacco**

Burley supplies about 10 percent of the world's tobacco production. There is a dizzying assortment of varieties. Important to the commercial grower, their differences are in the growing time, yield of the leaves and flavor and disease resistance. In addition to flavor and yield, commercial tobacco farmers need to take into consideration resistance to black shank, blue mold, insects such as aphids, hornworm, and budworm.

For our purposes, the heirloom varieties are readily obtainable. What the varieties have in common are similar flowers and their leaves turn to a golden yellow at the end of the season. They are all lightly scented. I have found them to be excellent butterfly and hummingbird attractors. The different heirloom varieties, readily obtainable, are: KY-14, KY-17, KY-907, TN-86, TN-90, VA-509,

TA-16, and the most common is TA-14, which is a good type for first-time growers.

Commercial Varieties are hybrids that include the following types: HB 4488PLC; KY 212LC; KT 209LC; KT 210LC; KY 206LC; KT 200LC; and scores of others. The APPENDIX includes a comprehensive list of all varieties of tobacco that I culled and compiled from thousands of documents. Many of them are no longer available, but I have listed for those readers who are interested in historical research.

Commercial hybrids are generally sold pelletized. Although commercial tobacco is beyond the scope of this book, for those readers who are interested in learning more, www.rickardseed.com or www.crosscreekseeds.com have a wealth of information.

Sources:
Rickard Seeds
Cross Creek Seed

CIMARRON

Photo: Daggawalla Seeds © **Cimarron Tobacco**

Common Names: Cimarron; Solaniflora

Binominal Name: Nicotiana tabacum solaniflora

A very rare native tobacco found in the lowlands of Chile. It is a perennial that blooms in its second year. It thrives in arid conditions, often without rain for three to five months. Full sun is recommended. Cimarron is sensitive to freezing and is recommended for USDA Zones 10 and 11. The green, five-petal flowers are on branching stalks that reach a height of up to 60 inches. The leaves are thick and short. Note the unusual wavy edges.

Sources:
Daggawalla
Chileflora.com

CLEVELANDII

Photo: Wikipedia NPS **Clevelandii Tobacco Flower**

Common Name: Cleveland's Tobacco; Clevelandii

Binominal Name: Nicotiana tabacum clevelandii

Once cultivated by Native Americans in the Southwestern United States, it is drought and cold resistant and fast blooming. Grows in poor, rocky soil. Trumpet-shaped, white flowers show about three weeks after transplanting and bloom all summer long. Now found in Arizona and parts of California, but as it fell out of favor, the distribution dropped. Interestingly, adding to the plant's mystery, it is found in a very small area of Victoria, Australia.

Photo: Wikipedia NPS **Clevelandii Tobacco**

Sources:
New Hope
Northwood Seeds
Victory Seeds

COMSTOCK SPANISH

Photo: northwoodseeds.com © **Comstock Spanish Tobacco**

Common Name: Comstock Spanish

Binominal Name: Nicotiana tabacum comstock spanish

Comstock Spanish is an interesting variety with its roots in the history of Wisconsin. Pioneering farmers from the East had trouble adapting to the wide-open prairies of Wisconsin. They were accustomed to farming at the edge of forests clearings and struggled to find the crops and methods that would succeed in the open spaces and harsh winters of Wisconsin.

Tobacco farming was first tried about 1850 and was a commercial success. Comstock was developed from seeds obtained from the Connecticut Valley. The tobacco was suitable for cigars and found a ready market with the large and growing cigar-smoking German population of Wisconsin. As recently as 1950, there were still over 6,000 farms raising tobacco in Wisconsin.

In addition to soil and conditions that were suitable, cow manure was plentiful. It was a win-win situation for Wisconsin's farmers and stockmen.

For our criteria, Comstock Spanish as a cigar tobacco is raised primarily for its large leaves. The leaves also tend to arch upward in a columnar appearance. Clusters of pink/red flowers are butterfly attractors. It reaches about 48 inches high. Space the plants 18–24 inches apart. It will thrive in full sun in various soil types but needs to be fertilized regularly.

Sources:
Northwood Seeds
New Hope
West Seed Farm

CONNECTICUT TOBACCOS

Photo: northwoodseeds.com © **Connecticut Shadeleaf Tobacco**

Common Names: Connecticut Broadleaf, Shadeleaf, or Wrapper

Grown in the Connecticut River Valley since the early 1800s, the leaf has a well-earned international reputation. It was even used to bind Havana cigars until the embargo of Cuba cut off their supply. The unique soil, climate, and know-how of the valley farmers, not to mention the vast supply of sheep fertilizer that was available, started an industry that, even though it has shrunk (30,800 acres in 1921 to 2,000 today), still operates.

If you are traveling through the Hartford Connecticut area, do not miss an opportunity to visit the Luddy/Taylor Connecticut Valley Tobacco Museum. Tel. 806-285-1888. For hours and directions, visit www.tobaccohistsoc.org.

Today's Connecticut tobaccos were developed from strains of Sumatra tobacco. Sumatra tobacco began to be imported in the late 1880s. The high-quality leaf began to supplant what was currently being raised and sold by the Connecticut farmers to cigar manufacturers. With Yankee ingenuity, the local farmers devised an enclosure made of cloth that would duplicate the light and humidity of Sumatra. It worked splendidly and soon shade tents covered the landscape of the valley. The shade tent method is still used today. Because any damage to the leaf would leave it useless as a cigar wrapper, an inordinate amount of care is needed in the handling. It is a very labor-intensive farm product.

Growing up to 72 inches high, the leaves are about 30 inches long by 16 inches wide. Topped by clusters of pink flowers. They need frequent watering and fertilizer for the best growth. Can tolerate shade very well. An excellent indoors plant.

Connecticut Shadeleaf Tent

Inevitably, when you mention you have tobacco plants in your garden, someone is going to ask, "Do you have Connecticut cigar wrapper tobacco?"

Answer in the affirmative.

Sources:
Connecticut 49: Northwood Seeds
Connecticut Broadleaf: New Hope; Northwood Seeds; Sustainable Seeds; The Tobacco Seed Co., UK; Victory Seeds; West Seed Farm
Connecticut Shade: B&T; New Hope; Northwood Seeds
Connecticut Wrapper: Adaptive Seeds

*Maintaining and harvesting Connecticut Shade tobacco is extremely la-
bor intensive. With over 16,000 acres under cultivation in the 1940s,
migrant student labor was recruited from the South. Among the tobacco
plants were the seeds of the civil rights movement.*

*In the summer of 1944, a young Martin Luther King Jr. worked at
the Simsbury tobacco farm of Cullman Brothers, Inc. Like many other African American students from the South who came to work in
Connecticut's fields, he hoped to earn money for school and his family.*

*King's letters home to his mother and father reveal a fifteen-year-old's
astonishment at the prospects open to African Americans in the compar-
atively less restrictive North. He wrote of worshiping alongside whites in
a Simsbury church and of dining in Hartford. "I never though[t] that
a person of my race could eat anywhere," he wrote, "but we…ate in one
of the finest restaurant[s].…" The state was not free of racism, of course,
but the lack of overt segregation, such as King experienced in the South,
made a lasting impression.*

*Years later, in his autobiography, King observed that his experiences
in Connecticut and during the train ride back home to Atlanta helped
heighten his awareness of the cruel injustice of segregation:*

> *After that summer in Connecticut, it was a bitter feeling going back
> to segregation. It was hard to understand why I could ride wherever
> I pleased on the train from New York to Washington and then had to
> change to a Jim Crow car at the nation's capital in order to continue
> the trip to Atlanta. The first time that I was seated behind a curtain
> in a dining car, I felt as if the curtain had been dropped on my self-
> hood. I could never adjust to the separate waiting rooms, separate eat-
> ing places, separate rest rooms, partly because the separate was always
> unequal, and partly because the very idea of separation did something
> to my sense of dignity and self-respect.[1]*

---

[1] http://connecticuthistory.org/dr-kings-dream-had -roots-in-connecticut/

What if Connecticut had not become the center of highly demanded shade tobacco? What if the hand labor needed to harvest the crop had not brought Martin Luther King Jr. north to be exposed to a degree of freedom he could never experience in the South and could never again accept as "normal?"

How different our history of racial justice might have been without men like him. How different without tobacco.

COYOTE

Photo: USDI BLM **Coyote Tobacco Flower**

Common Names: Coyote tobacco; Mountain Tobacco; Attenuata

Binominal Name: Nicotiana tabacum attenuata

Found in nature from British Columbia to Texas. Coyote tobacco is a hardy annual that self seeds for the following season. Early prospectors dubbed it Coyote Tobacco. It is a foul smelling plant with long, branching stems ending in white or greenish flowers that are 1 to 2 inches long at the end of long, slender tubes. The flowers open in the evening. The basal leaves are 2 to 6 inches long. Coyote tobacco is common at higher elevations in arid conditions and poor soil.

Photo: USDI BLM **Coyote Tobacco Plant**

Sources:
Daggawalla
Allies

CRIOLLA

*Photo: northwoodseeds.com © **Criollo 98 Tobacco***

Criollo is primarily used in the making of cigars. It was, by most accounts, one of the original Cuban tobaccos that emerged around the time of Columbus. The term means "native seed," and thus, a tobacco variety using the term such as Dominican Criollo may or may not have anything to do with the original Cuban seed nor the recent hybrid, Criollo 98.

Wikipedia: Criollo Tobacco

Common Name: Criollo; Criollo 98

Binominal Name: nicotiana tabacum criollo

There is a mystery that surrounds this particular variety of nicotiana. It may or may not have its roots in the bundles of tobacco that Columbus's "Indians" gave as peace offerings to the sailors aboard the Nina, Pinta, and the Santa Maria—bundles of leaves that they promptly tossed aside, having no idea why they were being offered to them.

Two of Columbus's sailors while on an overland expedition in Cuba, were introduced to the proper use of these leaves. Shortly after, the habit swept through Europe.

For our use, the plants have cluster of pink flowers that are excellent butterfly and hummingbird attractors. The plants reach 72 inches high with broad, long leaves reaching 36 inches long. The Criollo 98 has slightly shorter leaves but is grown for its greater resistance to diseases. Plant it in loose loam with regular fertilizing. Space the plants 12–16 inches apart.

Sources:
Criollo:
Heirloom Tobacco
Sustainable Seeds
The Tobacco Seed Co., UK

Criollo 98:
Northwood Seeds
Virginia Tobacco Seeds, Spain

DAULE

Photo: Beth B. Pocker © **Daule Tobacco Flower**

Common Name: Daule

Binominal Name: Nicotiana tabacum daule

Found only in the region of the Daule River in Ecuador, this is a rare plant with leaves that have high nicotine content, so please handle with care. Daule grows on sturdy stalks to about 36 inches high. The leaves are about 20 inches long and 8 inches wide and thick. It tolerates a wide range of soil but needs full sun. Topped with a cluster of pink flowers.

Photo: Beth B. Pocker © **Daule Tobacco**

Sources:
Heirloom Tobacco
Northwood
Sustainable Seeds

DELGOLD

Photo: northwoodseeds.com ©

Common Name: Delgold

The pride of Canada! Delgold was developed in Ontario in 1980 by crossing nicotiana rustica and two American varieties, Hicks Broadleaf and Virginia 115. The result was a tobacco high in nicotine but with larger leaves, thus a higher yield per acre.

It was a commercial success. For our purposes, we have a unique cultivar for our gardens. It is fast growing, tall sturdy column, about 72 to 90 inches high with large leaves and clusters of pink flowers that are hummingbird and butterfly attractors. The leaves are about 18 inches long and 12 inches wide. It also hardy and tolerates a minor amount of frost. Because of its high nicotine content, handle the leaves with care.

Sources:
Northwood Seeds
B&T
Sustainable Seeds
Nicky's, UK only
The Tobacco Seed Co., UK

DESERT

Photo: Courtesy of Dale. A. Zimmerman Herbarium ©
Desert Tobacco Trigonophylla

Common Names: Desert Tobacco; Obtusifolia; Trigonophylla

Binominal Names: Nicotiana tabacum trigonophylla or Nicotiana tabacum obtusifolia

Synonym: Nicotiana tabacum obtusifolia

This plant was the bane of stockmen from California to Texas. Highly toxic, it made cattle sick when grazing in grasslands. Native Americans and cowboys alike smoked the dried leaves.

Desert tobacco is found along canyon walls and rocky mesas. It is a perennial that sends leafy stems from a crown root and ends in tubular white flowers that are about 1-inch long, tinged with green. It is an excellent butterfly attractor. The flowers are open during the daytime. The leaves at the base are oval to egg-shape while the upper leaves are long and narrow. It can grow up to 36 inches tall. Desert tobacco requires little watering and tolerates poor rocky soil. This is an excellent choice for rock gardens. It thrives in full sun. They do not tolerate cold, and in warmer climes, they will be evergreens.

Photo: Wikipedia **Obtusifolia Tobacco Flower**

Photo: Richard Pocker © **Desert Tobacco**

Sources:
Horizon Herbs
Heavenly Products

DIXIE SHADE

Photo: Westseed Farm © **Dixie Shade Tobacco**

Common Name: Dixie Shade

Florida and Georgia tobacco farming began prior to the Civil War. Facing similar conditions to the farmers in the Connecticut Valley (see Connecticut Tobaccos) over the increasing imports of Sumatra tobacco for cigar wrappers, they began to experiment in growing tobacco under tents of special cloth that helped to duplicate the light and humidity of Sumatra. The shades worked and reversed the failing fortunes of the Georgian and Florida tobacco farmer.

Released in 1958, Dixie Shade was the result of those experiments. What we have is a large leaf tobacco plant with light-green leaves. The leaves are about 30 inches long and 16 inches wide. It grows to about 60 to 72 inches tall. Dixie Shade has clusters of pink flowers. Space the plants about 24 inches apart. As with other shade tobaccos, Dixie Shade requires well-drained soil and regular fertilizer to produce large plants.

Sources:
New Hope
West Seed Farm

Before the invention of the corrugated box, there was the barrel.

From the time of the Roman Empire, through the 1940s the wood barrel with its arched, bulging sides, proved to be the strongest container for shipping and storage. Easily filled, sealed, and tipped on its side, a man could roll a tremendous weight unassisted for short distances. The shape of a wood barrel is nothing more than a container with its own built-in wheel.

Various commodities, both wet and dry, were placed in specialized barrels, and each barrel given its own moniker, based upon its size and use; be it for fish, beer, wine, tobacco, or gunpowder or any other commodity.

Barrel capacities were set by royal decree over the course of time. A barrel of salmon or beer might measure 42 gallons while one of cod or honey would be 32 gallons. With time, the measure of a fish barrel would be 38 gallons while a keg of gunpowder became standardized at 100 pounds.

Hogshead is one of the many arcane terms of length or volume measurement, such as the rod, cubit, peck, tun, butt, pipe, puncheon, priggin, firkin, keeve, cask, vat and tan whose origins have been lost to history. So has the name of the inventor of the first barrel.

Tobacco was charged transportation by the hogshead. A hogshead was considered a particular size, not weight, and the enforcement of standards was extremely lax. The pragmatic colonist soon began to fidget with the dimensions, intending to ship as much tobacco as possible at the lowest price.

Originally, the size of the hogshead was set by statue in 1423 in England at 63 gallons (approximately 30 inches wide by 48 inches high). In the hands of the tobacco farmer, they soon began to bulge (pun intended). Under the thrifty colonists, the barrels began to grow until they became large enough to handle one thousand pound of tobacco.

Barrel makers, called coopers, were found in every village. Itinerant coopers found constant employment and traveled from farm to farm with their tools as needed.

The average tobacco farmer might have three to four acres under cultivation; he needed ten times that amount of property for timber to have enough wood on hand to produce barrel staves.

As tobacco farmers depleted the soil in coastal areas, they were forced to move inland in search of new ground. A need for a specialist in transportation arose. Wagoners and teamsters were the foundation of the commercial transportation industry in America, shipping thousands upon thousands of hogsheads of tobacco and every imaginable product as the nation grew.

FLORIDA SUMATRA

Photo: northwoodseeds.com © **Florida Sumatra Tobacco**

Common Name: Florida Sumatra

Tobacco has its historical ties to Florida tobacco farmers that pre-date the Civil War. Sumatra is found in catalogs as far back as 1884. Although the tides of fortune and fickle tastes of the tobacco market have caused boom and bust years, this variety has survived to become the most planted and popular of homegrown heirloom types.

Primarily raised as a cigar tobacco, the leaves are large, about 24 inches long by 15 inches wide and fast growing as it matures in fifty-five days. Topped with a cluster of pink flowers, the leaves emanate a delicious smell, described by some people as "spicy."

This plant thrives in full sun but will tolerate shade very well. It grows to about 72 inches tall.

Sources:
New Hope
Northwood Seeds
West Seed Farm

GLUTINOSA

Photo: Courtesy of Laurie Bousalt © **Glutinosa Tobacco Flower**

Common Names: Glutinosa; Big Mouth; Peach Screamer

Binominal Name: Nicotiana tabacum glutinosa

It is difficult to use the words "charming" and "tobacco" in one sentence. I will make an exception in this case. Linnaeus classified Glutinosa in 1753. It is a native nicotiana of Bolivia and Peru.

Growing about to about 24 inches high, it has an abundance of peach-pink, star-faced, bell-shaped flowers about 1 inch across with wide-open mouths that are spectacular and great hummingbird attractors. The leaves are ovate shape about 24 inches long on the bottom row. They require full sun in loose loam to sandy soil.

A unique nicotiana that is easy to grow and with abundant sources for seeds. It is a good beginner's plant.

Photo: Courtesy of Laurie Bousalt © **Glutinosa Tobacco Plant**

Sources:
Impecta, Sweden
JL Hudson
Nicky's, UK only
Silene, Belgium
The Flower Company (plants only)
Virginia Tobacco Seeds, Spain
B&T

HAVANA TOBACCOS

Photo: Richard Pocker © **Havana 142 Tobacco Flower**

Common Names: Havana; Havana 142; Havana 608; Havana 501, Havana 263; Habano;
Havana Z299; Habano 2000

Havana is one of the fastest and easiest to grow heirloom nicotiana. Bred for the leaves, on this variety they are huge. The clusters of pink flowers are excellent hummingbird and butterfly attractors.

The different varieties may be chosen for the taste of the leaves or maturity time, but for our purposes, the appearances are all very similar. The plants have fairly sturdy stalks but may require staking in windy conditions. They average 72 to 90 inches high with leaves that reach 36 inches long and 12 inches wide. Havanas require watering, full sun, loose loam soil, and regular fertilizer. Space them out at 24 inches apart for best growth. They do not tolerate cold conditions.

In a large container, they are spectacular for the patio or deck. The Havanas will also make spectacular indoor plants.

Photo: Richard Pocker © **Havana 142 Tobacco**

Sources:
Habano:
Heirloom Tobacco

Habano 2000:
Northwood Seeds
Sustainable Seeds

Havana:
Cibergarden, Spain

Havana 142:
B&T
JL Hudson
Northwood Seeds
Sustainable Seeds
The Tobacco Seed Co., UK

Havana 263:
New Hope
Havana 608:
B&T
JL Hudson
Northwood Seeds
Sustainable Seeds

Havana Z299:
Sustainable Seeds
Northwood Seeds

INDIAN

Photo: National Park Service **Indian Tobacco Flower**

Common Names: Indian Tobacco; Quadrivalvis

Binominal Name: Nicotiana tabacum quadrivalvis

This is the parent plant of Bigelovii (nicotiana quadrivalvis var. bigelovii). Quadrivalvis is native to the western United States. In fact, in appearance, it is so close that a study of the two varieties in 1912 was done that determined that the differences in the two plants mainly resided in the seed chambers.[2] Some botanists consider it a synonym for Bigelovii.

What we have is a sprawling annual that grows up to 72 inches high. Thin leaves surround the base, and the array of flowers range from white-green to a purple tinge, and the five-petal face may be up to two inches across.

---

[2] E.M. East, "A Study of Hybrids between Nicotiana Bigelovii and N. quadrivalvis," *Botanical Gazette* 53, no. 3 (Mar., 1912): 243–248

Thrives best in semiarid conditions in many types of soil. It is an interesting addition to the garden.

Photo: National Park Service **Indian Tobacco**

Source:
Northwood Seeds
Sustainable Seeds

IZMIR

Photo: northwoodseeds.com © **Izmir Ozbis Tobacco Flower**

Common Names: Izmir; Turkish Izmir; Izmir Ozbis; Lebanese Izmir

A unique narrow, columnar appearance with small uniform leaves. Izmir is suitable for tight spaces. Izmir is classified as an Oriental tobacco, grown for its strong flavor. The Lebanese variety is not fully classified, but it grows taller, 72 inches as compared to the Turkish variety at 60 inches, and matures in only fifty days versus seventy to eighty for the Turkish. Otherwise, aside from the color differences of the beautiful flowers, the plants look very similar. Space apart at 12–16 inches in loose loam to sandy soil. Full sun and water well.

Photo: northwoodseeds.com © **Izmir Lebanese Tobacco Flower**

Sources:
Izmir Lebanese:
Northwood Seeds

Izmir Ozbis:
Northwood Seeds
Sustainable Seeds

Izmir:
Cibergarden, Spain
Virginia Tobacco Seeds, Spain
The Tobacco Seed Co., UK

JASMINE

Photo Richard Pocker © **Jasmine Tobacco**

Common Names: Jasmine; Sweet Scented

Binominal Name: Nicotiana tabacum alata or affinis var. grandiflora

Jasmine is a very popular variety of nicotiana. Large, white, trumpet-shaped flowers that are the most heavily scented nicotiana. Be sure to plant some near an open window in the ground or in containers. It is also very easy to grow. It is a good choice for the beginner. Perfect for growing as a houseplant too. It grows 36 to 48 inches tall with short and narrow leaves. Plant them 12–16 inches apart in full sun to partial shade. The soils should be loose loam to sandy, and they do not require frequent watering.

The blooms start midsummer and last through the fall. The leaves are narrow and long.

This plant has been awarded the Royal Horticultural Society Award of Garden Merit.

Sources:
Select Seeds
The Flower Company (plants only)
Allies
B&T
Diane's Seeds
JL Hudson
Northwood Seeds
Seedaholic
Seedman.com (UK only)
Special Plants, UK
Terroir Seeds
Sustainable Seeds
Victory Seeds

KNIGHTIANA

Photo: Special Plants, UK © **Knightiana Tobacco**

Common Names: Knightiana; Green Tears

Binominal Name: Nicotiana tabacum knightiana

Another of that rare nicotiana that exhibits so much charm, it is hard to believe it's a tobacco. It is distinctive from Langsdorfii as the flowers are smaller, two-toned green, tubular-shaped, and dusted with a powdery white cast.

The stems are branching and reach 48–60 inches. The plant thrives in full sun to partial shade in a loose loam soil. Moderate watering required. An excellent container plant too.

Photo: Special Plants, UK © **Knightiana in a English Country Garden**

Sources:
B&T
Hazzard's Seed Store
Plant World Seeds, UK
Portland Nursery (plants only)
Seedman.com (UK only)
Silene, Belgium
Special Plants, UK
The Flower Company (plants only)

Most products produced from nature are neither all good nor all evil.

Just as the poppy produces heroin and morphine, one is the scourge of humanity and the other the savior.

It is indisputable that tobacco kills millions of people every year and causes untold misery to the sufferer and the friends and families they leave behind. Yet scientists are discovering that the plant can play a vital role in the production of vaccines and drugs because of its high biomass and rapid growth. Discoveries abound in the field of producing engineered forms of artemisinin, a compound that is vital in the worldwide fight against malaria.

Over 250 million new cases of malaria occur every year. Untreated it becomes life threatening. Producing enough artemisinin is imperative in this fight. Tobacco can now save lives.

Not only is tobacco in the fight against malaria, it is used to produce vaccines against anthrax and swine flu, and there are trials to produce vaccines using modified tobacco plants to fight norovirus, the "cruise ship virus" that causes gastrointestinal illness that fells 75 million people a year. It is also playing a part in developing a vaccine for Ebola.

Tobacco-gown insulin is in the testing stages too.

Using genetically modified tobacco plants, pheromones can be produced that can be used to trap pests, thereby reducing the need for spraying.

The benefit of using genetically modified tobacco as a medium for producing these drugs as opposed to corn or another food plant is that tobacco is not usually found in the food chain, thereby reducing the possibility of ingestion.

While tobacco is hardly a panacea, the ongoing research promises to benefit world health at a much-reduced cost for drug therapies. Unaffordable therapies for the world's poorest populations will come within reach.

LANGSDORFII

Photo: Richard Pocker © **Langsdorfii Tobacco Flower**

Common Names: Chilean Tobacco; Lemon Tree Tobacco; Langsdorfii

Binominal Name: Nicotiana tabacum langsdorfii

This heirloom nicotiana was discovered in the area of Chile/Brazil in the early nineteenth century. It is quick growing on slender stalks with clusters of apple-green, drooping, bell-shaped flowers. The leaves cluster at the bottom of the plant, leaving the 2-inch long hummingbird attractors dangling in free space. The plants are generally 36 inches tall but can grow to 60 inches. They are excellent for planters both indoors and out. It is easy to grow and a very showy beginner's plant. Space plants about 16 inches apart in well-drained soil. Requires full sun to partial shade.

Langsdorfii are annuals, but in warmer climes, they will self-seed the following spring.

An interesting variation of Langsdorfii is Langsdorfii Cream-Splash. It is slightly bushier in appearance, and the wavy leaves are edged in a cream color.

Photo: plant-world-seeds.com © **Langsdorfii Creame Splash**

Sources: Langdorfii
B&T
Baker Creek
Botanical Interests
De Werkplaats, Netherlands
Hardy Plants
Hazzard's Seed Store
Plant World Seeds, UK
Portland Nursery (plants only)
Seedman.com (UK only)
Select Seeds
Silene, Belgium
Special Plants, UK
Sustainable Seeds

Swallowtail
Terroir Seeds
The Flower Company (plants only)
Thompson & Morgan, US & UK
White Flower Farms (plants only)
Chiltern, UK
Hazzard's Seed Store
Impecta, Sweden
Von Trapp Greenhouse (plants only)

Sources: Langsdorfii Creame Splash
Plant World Seeds, UK
B&T
Nicky's, UK
Chiltern, UK

LIME GREEN TOBACCO

Photo: Richard Pocker © **Lime Green Tobacco**

Common Names: Alata Lime Green; Affinis Lime Green; Persian Lime Green

Binominal Name: Nicotiana tabacum affinis var. lime green

Also known as Persian or Iranian tobacco, this variation, with its massive clusters of lime-green, trumpet-shaped tubes ending with a five-pointed star, is an unusual addition to any garden. As the photo below illustrates, it is also an excellent variety to add to a planter. A great cut flower too.

It is an heirloom variety. I was able to collect the seeds from the above street planters (with permission) at the end of the season and successfully plant the seeds the following spring.

They are relatively short; most are around 30 inches in height but can reach 60 inches. Plant them about 20 inches apart in loose loam in full to partial shade. They are wonderful butterfly and hummingbird attractors.

Photo: Richard Pocker ©
Lime Green in Street Planter New Canaan Connecticut

Sources:
Baker Creek
B&T
Chiltern, UK
De Werkplaats, Netherlands

DT Brown, UK
Hardy Plants
Hazzard's Seed Store
Impecta, Sweden
Nicky's, UK
Nuts n Cones, UK
Sarah Raven, UK
Seedaholic
Seedman.com (UK only)
Silene, Belgium
Special Plants, UK
The Flower Company (plants only)

LITTLE CRITTENDEN

Photo: Terroir Seeds © **Little Crittenden Tobacco**

Common Name: Little Crittenden

Binominal Name: Nicotiana tabcum little crittenden

This variety dates back from the 1880s from Crittenden County, Kentucky. The stalks of this variety are rigid for a straight plant with unique long and narrow leaves that are crinkled and somewhat coarse. It grows to 36 inches on very rigid, straight stalks. There are clusters of pink flowers. Plant in full sun about 16 inches apart in loose soil. It is also an excellent container plant due to its shorter height.

Sources:
JL Hudson
Sustainable Seeds
Terroir Seeds
The Tobacco Seed Co., UK

LITTLE DUTCH

Photo: Richard Pocker © **Little Dutch Tobacco**

Common Name: Little Dutch

Binominal name: Nicotiana tabacum little dutch

Little Dutch is another choice nicotiana for medium size plant-ers. It is relatively small among heirloom nicotiana and grows on sturdy stalks to 36 inches tall with abundant narrow leaves 16 to 19 inches long and topped with clusters of pink flowers. It has a sweet fragrant scent at night. Plant about 16 inches apart in loose soil in full sun. As a cut flower, it will maintain its scent indoors.

First imported from Germany about 1880, it was raised in the Miami Valley area of Ohio as a cigar tobacco but fell out of favor, and now is rarely seen in the field, but we have it as a wonderful garden addition.

Sources:
Heirloom Tobacco
New Hope
Northwood Seeds
Sustainable Seeds
Victory Seeds
Virginia Tobacco Seeds, Spain

LIZARD TAIL ORINOCO

Photo: Richard Pocker © **Lizard Tail Orinoco Tobacco**

Common Name: Lizard Tail Orinoco

Binominal name: Nicotiana tabacum orinoco var. lizard tail

What do a lizard tail and a tobacco leaf have in common? After raising this nicotiana for several seasons, I still don't have the answer, but I like it for its bold appearance. The stalk is upright with long, tapering leaves that at a stretch might hint at the reptile tail, but the origins of the name are lost to history.

Standing almost 72 inches high, Lizard Tail Orinoco is topped with a cluster of pink flowers. It is easy to grow, and as you can see from the photo, it works well in a large container. Plant in full sun, loose soil, and space 16–20 inches apart. Lizard Tail Orinoco is another excellent butterfly and hummingbird attractor.

Sources:
B&T
JL Hudson
New Hope
The Tobacco Seed Co., UK
West Seed Farm

MADOLE TOBACCOS

Photo: northwoodseeds.com © **Madole Tobacco**

Common Names: Madole; Improved Madole; Narrow Leaf Madole; Tom Ross Madole

An heirloom type nicotiana, grouped together for our gardening purposes. They are often the choice of commercial growers for the various disease resistance or maturity properties they offer. They are all classified as "dark" tobacco for the color of the leaf after it has cured.

Most of them grow to about 48 inches tall on study stalks with leaves of 16–18 inches long. Leaves have a fuzzy texture. Clusters of pink flowers.

Sources: Madole
Northwood Seeds
Heirloom Tobacco
New Hope
Semena-Osvia Slovakia
Sustainable Seeds

Sources: Madole Improved
B&T
JL Hudson
West Seed Farm

Sources: Madole Tom Ross
B&T
JL Hudson

MAMMOTH

White Mammoth Tobacco

I grew White Mammoth last year. Give it the right conditions and you'll know why they have "mammoth" in the name. One stand-alone plant I grew reached 8' tall (top of the flowers) and had leaf 36"+ long and 24" = wide, monsters. The stalk at the base at the end of the season was a good 1 ½ wide or more.
Will Greenwald; Chilliwick BC

Common Names: Black Mammoth; White Mammoth; Yellow Mammoth

Greenwald has said it best. If you have space and want a monster tobacco plant, Mammoth is the choice. They all mature fairly rapidly and vary slightly in size. Classified as "brightleaf" tobaccos for the color of the leaf after curing, they have clusters of pink flowers and are worth experimenting with if you have the space.

One variety of Mammoth that seems to have disappeared, Maryland Mammoth, was the subject of intensive experiments in the 1920s regarding photoperiodism, the study of why certain plants flower during long days and others during shorter period of sunlight. Apparently, Maryland Mammoth did not bloom until the shorter days of late fall arrived.

Mammoths tend to have thick stalks at the base of the plant. The leaves can reach 36 inches long and 24 inches wide. Plant 24–36 inches apart in loose loam.

Sources: Black Mammoth
JL Hudson
The Tobacco Seed Co., UK

Source: White Mammoth
Northwood Seeds
West Seed Farm
Source: Yellow Mammoth
New Hope
West Seed Farm

MARITIMA

Photo: Wikimedia Commons **Maritima Tobacco**

Common Names: Australian Coast, Coast Tobacco, or Maritima

This nicotiana is a native heirloom tobacco found in South Australia in sandy or rocky soil along the coast. It is a rare but beautiful plant with small white trumpet like flowers on thin branching stalks. The leaves are basal and ovate. It is used by the Aboriginal Australians. Plant in full sun and tolerates dry conditions and poor soil.

In the wild, Maritima tobacco reaches 40 inches high.

Sources:
Chiltern, UK
Daggawalla
Silene, Belgium

MARYLAND TOBACCO

Photo: Wikimedia © **Maryland Type Tobacco Field**

Common Names: Catterton; MD 609; MD A30; Keller tobacco

Maryland tobaccos are another variety grown by commercial tobacco farmers for their distinctive flavor and disease resistance.

For the gardener, they have a distinctive pyramid shape with large,
pointed leaves. Some of these varieties can trace their lineage back
almost 400 years. They are becoming rare, as cigarette companies
have discontinued using many of Maryland types. Space them 16–
20 inches apart in loose loam and water frequently. They are fast
maturing and disease resistant.

Sources:
Catterton-Northwood Seeds
Catterton-The Tobacco Seed Co., UK

Catterton-Victory Seeds
Catterton-Virginia Tobacco Seeds, Spain
Catterton-West Seed Farm
Maryland-The Tobacco Seed Co., UK
Maryland—Keller-West Seed Farm
Maryland—Keller-New Hope
MD 609-Virginia Tobacco Seeds, Spain
MD 609-Northwood Seeds
MD 609-Sustainable Seeds
MD A30-Northwood Seeds
MD A30-Sustainable Seeds

MONTE CALME YELLOW

Photo: northwoodseeds.com © **Monte Calme Yellow Tobacco**

Common Name: Monte Calme Yellow; Monte Calme Blonde

Monte Calme Yellow grows to 60–72 inches with twelve to fourteen, huge, eye-catching leaves, 30 inches long and 24 inches wide. The leaves are dark green with light-colored stems.

Clusters of pink flowers. The plant has a resistance to light frosts. Plant in full sun about 20–24 inches apart in loose loam. Water frequently.

Sources:
Virginia Tobacco Seeds, Spain
Northwood Seeds
The Tobacco Seed Co., UK
Sustainable Seeds

MOUNTAIN PIMA

Photo: northwoodseeds.com © **Mountain Pima Tobacco**

Common Name: Mountain Pima; Mount Pima

Mountain Pima is another nicotiana wrapped in an enigma. Classified as a rustica, it has pink leaves instead of the usual yellow of that type. It has large pointed leaves and is used as a smoking tobacco. Some experts classify it as a nicotiana tabacum.

Originally grown by the Pima Indians in the Gila River area of what is now Arizona, as a ceremonial tobacco, it took the arrival of the Spanish to convince them that smoking was an everyday pleasure. The Conquistadors taught them the same thing about alcohol. They also left plenty of diseases unknown to the Pima prior to the arrival of the European. Overall, it was a bad bargain.

But what we have is and interesting rustica nicotiana for our garden. It only reaches 36 to 48 inches high, and it is very hardy. It will self-seed in warmer climes and tolerates a wide range of soils.

Sources:
Northwood Seeds
Victory Seeds
Native Seeds
Sustainable Seeds

MUTABILIS

Photo: Special Plants, UK © **Mutabilis Tobacco Flower**

Common Names: Mutabilis; Marshmallow; Flowering

Binominal Name: Nicotiana tabacum mutabilis

Blooming from July to September, this is one of the most beautiful of the flowering heirloom tobaccos. It can reach 48 to 60 inches high. The stalks are thin and branching. Space the plants about 16 inches apart. Mutabilis has abundant trumpet-shaped flowers with colors that range from rose to pink, purple, and white; hence, the name mutabilis is derived from Latin word for *changeable*. The flowers are perfect for cutting and arranging in a vase. They are also excellent for containers as well as the garden. It is an excellent beginner's plant too. A wonderful butterfly and hummingbird attractor.

Photo: Daggawalla Seeds © **Mutabilis Tobacco**

Sources:
Special Plants, UK
Burpee
Chiltern, UK
Daggawalla
De Werkplaats Netherlands
Hazzard's Seed Store
Impecta, Sweden
Portland Nursery (plants only)
Seedman.com (UK only)
Silene, Belgium
B&T
Thompson & Morgan, US & UK

ONE SUCKER

Photo: northwoodseeds.com © **One Sucker Tobacco**

Common Name: One Sucker; Ox Tongue or Tongue Tobacco

Suckers refer to branches that grow off the main stem of the tobacco plant. Suckers can sap the strength of the plant causing a
smaller number of leaves to grow or stunt the size of the plant.
Some varieties are more prone than other to grow them.

For an illustration of an extreme sucker, see the photo of **Yenidje**.
The sucker, running off to the left, is as large as the main stem.

Usually suckers are snapped off by hand, as they appear. Sometimes chemical sprays are used to control them. In the case of this variety, the tendency to grow them is genetically diminished.

Historically, it is believed that this variety came from what was commonly called Ox Tongue or Tongue tobacco, which is mentioned in medical/botany literature as far back as the late sixteenth century. At a stretch, as with Orinoco Lizard Tail tobacco, we can discern a vague resemblance. The dark-green, sharply pointed leaves can reach 36 inches in length. They have a crease down the center resembling a curled tongue.

With clusters of pink flowers and a height of 48–60 inches, it makes a very interesting addition to the garden or a large container. Planted in the garden, space them about 16 inches apart in loose loam

Sources:
JL Hudson
New Hope
Northwood Seeds
Sustainable Seeds
Victory Seeds
West Seed Farm

ORINOCO

Photo: northwoodseeds.com © **Orinoco Tobacco**

The Orinoco is one of the longest rivers in South America at 2,140 km (1,330 mi). Its drainage basin, sometimes called the Orinoquia, covers 880,000 square kilometers (340,000 sq. mi), with 76.3 percent of it in Venezuela and the remainder in Columbia. The Orinoco and its tributaries are the major transportation system for eastern and interior Venezuela and the Llanos of Colombia.
Source: Wikipedia

Common Names: Orinoco; Yellow Orinoco; White Stem Orinoco

Binominal Name: Nicotiana tabacum orinoco

It was John Rolfe who obtained seeds of this tobacco found in the Orinoco River basin in South America from the Spanish, either by trade or privateering. The seeds thrived in the rich soil surrounding the James River in Virginia and soon became the standard of European tobacco. It was so successful it assured the support of the fledging colony by the English Crown.

This plant assured the success of America.

It was possibly later supplanted by a strain of tobacco from Guatemala that became Virginia, the dominant variety that was exported to England.

What we have as Orinoco today is a descendant of that original plant. It stands about 72 inches high with long, narrow leaves about 24 inches long and 10 inches wide. Plant about 16–20 inches apart in loose loam. It requires full sun to partial shade.

True to its original ancestor, it has one of the highest nicotine contents of any tabacum. Handle the leaves with caution.

Sources:
Orinoco-Northwood Seeds
Orinoco-The Tobacco Seed Co., UK
Orinoco-Virginia Tobacco Seeds, Spain
Orinoco-Sustainable Seeds
White Stem Orinoco-New Hope
Yellow Orinoco-West Seed Farm

Patrick Henry's famous declaration, "Give me liberty, or give me death!" has rallied patriots through the ages. What is little known is that it had its roots in tobacco.

From almost the founding of the first Virginia colony at the beginning of the 1600s, tobacco was the primary source of income for the farmer. In exchange for being given monopoly status by the king of England, all tobacco had to be shipped to London where agents would determine the price they would pay. Terrible abuses soon surfaced, as middlemen would lend colonial farmers money in anticipation of amounts due on their tobacco. Farmers soon discovered the final price paid was far less than they had borrowed, and a crushing cycle of debt ensued.

The Crown also had a policy of prohibiting the circulation of coinage. Tobacco became the medium of exchange. If there were a surplus of crop and prices fell, there would be wild swings in value of what the farmer owed or could purchase.

In Virginia, it was local custom for the clergy to be paid approximately 18,000 pounds of tobacco a year as a salary. When prices were low, the farmer was anxious to meet their obligations by paying in tobacco. When prices were high, they looked for another remedy, as they would prefer to sell it in London for more money.

In 1758, the Virginia legislature passed a law called The Two Penny Law, giving the debtor the right to pay two cents a pound owed in cash. Of course, when prices were high, the clergy preferred to be paid in tobacco in order to sell it for the best price possible.

The clergy petitioned King George III to request he overturn what they felt was an unjust law. The king did so and Reverend James Murray, in 1759, brought suit to the Virginia court to recover what he felt was his lost wages.

It was this dispute that brought young (age twenty-seven) Patrick Henry to the fore.

Henry defended the farmers.

> *"Henry began his plea with hesitancy and awkwardness. His own father, who presided over the court, shrank in his chair, and the visiting clergymen glanced at one another in gestures of triumph.*

> *Then the young lawyer measured up to the opportunity, proving himself master of the art of arousing the passions of his hearers. In the words of one of his listeners, 'he made their blood run to cold and their hair to rise on end.' He refused to be bound by any narrow view of the case, summarizing the nature of the compact between king and people, declaring the law of 1758 a good law, which could not be vetoed, consistent with the compact. The king said Henry, instead of being a father, had now become a tyrant whose bad acts deserved no obedience. At these strong words, the murmur of 'Treason!' could be heard, but Henry paused not a moment in his argument.*"[3]

Perhaps we should not read too deeply into the initial foray of young Patrick Henry. As a decent litigator, he advocated and stated what needed to be said to win the case for his client. Independence was the furthest thing in his mind. He was a loyal Englishman, first and last.

But his words would burn bright. His argument would inspire Thomas Jefferson, who was fifteen years old at the time of the trial, eighteen years later in 1776, in drafting the Declaration of Independence. The great document, which stated the reasons "to dissolve the political bands that have connected them with another," imitated the demeanor of Henry's tobacco case.

---

[3] J.C. Robert, *The Story of Tobacco in America*, (New York: Alfred A. Knopf, 1949), 39.

PENNSYLVANIA RED

Photo: northwoodseeds.com © **Pennsylvania Red Tobacco**

Common Name: Pennsylvania Red

Pennsylvania Red is mentioned in seed catalogs as early as 1880. Grown for its distinctive flavor and large leaves. The name derives from the leaves that turn to a deep reddish brown when cured. It has clusters of pink flowers.

For our gardens, this is a fast-growing plant that matures in sixty-five to seventy days with long; dark leaves that reach up to 36 inches in length. Space them 24 inches apart in loose loam. Requires full sun.

Sources:
New Hope
Northwood Seeds
Sustainable Seeds
Virginia Tobacco Seeds, Spain
Seedman.com (UK only)

PERIQUE

Photo: Wikipedia ©
Perique Tobacco Flower

Common Name: Perique

Grown only in the Saint James Parish of Louisiana, it is considered the champagne of tobacco. Dating back to the early nineteenth century, it is still farmed by descendants of the original cultivators of Perique. At its peak, the Parish shipped twenty tons of this tobacco a year, and now less than sixteen acres are in cultivation. It is a strong, spicy tobacco used sparingly and blended with other types for pipe smokers.

The plants require early attention. They tend to produce a lot of suckers that need to be removed by hand (See **One Sucker and Yenidje**). The leaves are a dark, rich green. Clusters of pink flowers. The plants are about 30 inches high. Plant 16–20 inches apart in loose loam to sandy soil and in full sun.

Perique is a wonderful variety for planters or indoors.

Photo: Richard Pocker © **Perique Tobacco**

Sources:
B&T
Baker Creek
JL Hudson
New Hope
The Tobacco Seed Co., UK
Victory Seeds

PRENTINO

Photo. northwoodseeds.com © **Prentino Tobacco**

Common Name: Prentino

A native of Brazil, this rustica heirloom variety grows to about 48 inches tall on straight but flexible stalks with thin, delicate leaves. Prentino has clusters of pink flowers, which is unusual for a rustica that generally produces yellow ones. The leaves are thin and delicate, about 16 inches long and 7 inches wide. As most rusticas, in warmer climates this plant will self-seed for the following season.

It tolerates a wide range of soil. Plant them about 16 inches apart in full sun.

Prentino also produces many suckers (see **One Sucker**) that require removing by hand. It is a fast grower than matures in about forty-five days.

Photo: northwoodseeds.com © **Prentino Tobacco Leaf**

Sources:
Heirloom Tobacco
Sustainable Seeds
Northwood Seeds

RED RUSSIAN

Photo: northwoodseeds.com © **Red Russian Tobacco**

Common Name: Red Russian

Binominal Name: Nicotiana tabacum var. macrophylla purpurea

The history of this tobacco is a bit murky, but the results are spectacular. The USDA added the seeds to their collection in 1939. The sturdy stalks are about 36 to 48 inches high with dark-green leaves that are short and thick and somewhat rounded.

The flowers are one of the most spectacular of the nicotianas. They are large in size and maroon to pinkish in color. The blooms last all summer, and it is a terrific ornamental addition to our garden. Plant in loose loam, full sun, and space about 16 inches apart.

Sources:
Daggawalla
New Hope
Northwood Seeds
Sustainable Seeds
Victory Seeds
West Seed Farm

RUSTICA

Photo: Richard Pocker © **Rustica Tobacco Flower**

Common Names: Aztec; Indian Tobacco; Wild Tobacco; Sacred Tobacco; Mapacho; Thuoc Lao (Vietnam); Maxopka (Russia); see SOURCES for extensive list of common names.

The plant grows to about 36 inches high with many yellow flowers that open during the day. The leaves are slightly oblong and sticky. Because of its short height and fast growth, it will fill ground space. It is unique in its appearance among nicotiana. It is hardy and some varieties are grown as far north Alaska

There are many minor variations of this heirloom, native plant. Indian tribes in North and South America used it for centuries before it was introduced to the European explorers. Each tribe had its own distinct name for their tobacco.

What they all share in common is their yellow-green flowers and extremely high nicotine content. The leaves contain 9 percent nicotine compared to common smoking tobacco with 1–3 percent. Shamans used it to induce visions. In a powdered form, it was used as an excellent insecticide. It is cultivated worldwide for smoking and nicotine production. **Handle the leaves with caution.**

Space them about 20–24 inches apart. They tolerate a wide range of soils as long as it is well drained. Full sun is required.

Photo: Richard Pocker © **Rustica Tobacco**

Sources:
Rustica-Allies
Rustica-B&T
Rustica-Chiltern, UK
Rustica-Hardy Plants
Rustica-Impecta, Sweden
Rustica-Nicky's, UK only
Rustica-Plant World Seeds, UK
Rustica-Silene, Belgium
Rustica-The Tobacco Seed Co., UK
Rustica-Victory Seeds

Rustica-Virginia Tobacco Seeds, Spain
Rustica-Rostliny-Semena, Czech
Rustica-Aztec-Horizon Herbs
Rustica-Delaware Indian Sacred-Baker Creek
Rustica-Guarijio Makuchi-Native Seeds
Rustica-Hopi-Terroir Seeds
Rustica-Hopi-B&T
Rustica-Hopi-Baker Creek
Rustica-Hopi-Terroir Seeds
Rustica-Hopi-Horizon Herbs
Rustica-Hopi-Heavenly Products
Rustica-Hopley's-Special Plants, UK
Rustica-Indian-B&T
Rustica-Indian Black-Northwood Seeds
Rustica-Indian Black-Sustainable Seeds
Rustica-Isleta Pueblo-Native Seeds
Rustica-Isleta Pueblo-B&T
Rustica-Isleta Pueblo-Northwood Seeds
Rustica-Isleta Pueblo-The Tobacco Seed Co., UK
Rustica-Isleta Pueblo-Victory Seeds
Rustica-Kessu-Heirloom Tobacco
Rustica-Mopan Mayan-Heirloom Tobacco
Rustica-Mopan Mayan-Northwood Seeds
Rustica-Mopan Mayan-Sustainable Seeds
Rustica-Mohawk-Northwood Seeds
Rustica-Mohawk-Sustainable Seeds
Rustica-Mohawk-Victory Seeds
Rustica-Mapacho-Cibergarden, Spain
Rustica-Mapacho-Heavenly Products
Rustica-Papante-Native Seeds
Rustica-Punche-Northwood Seeds
Rustica-Punche-Sustainable Seeds
Rustica-Punche-B&T
Rustica-Punche -Native Seeds
Rustica-Sacred Cornplanter-Northwood Seeds

Rustica-Sacred Wyandot-Northwood Seeds
Rustica-San Juan-JL Hudson
Rustica-San Juan Pueblo-B&T
Rustica-Santo Domingo Ceremonial-Native Seeds
Rustica-Selesky-Semena-Osiva, Slovakia
Rustica-Southern Tepehuan-Native Seeds
Rustica-Tarahumara El Cuervo-Native Seeds
Rustica-Tarahumara Wild-Native Seeds
Rustica-Oneida-Horizon Herbs

Note:
If you are interested in ethnobotany or ethnology, an interesting book is a reprint of *Tobacco among the Kuruk Indians of California* by John P. Harrington published by the Smithsonian in 1932. It is available from J. L. Hudson. www.jlhudsonseeds.net, or write them at Box 337, LaHonda, CA 94020.

Another comprehensive book about the variations and uses of nicotiana rustica is *Tobacco Use by Native Americans* by Joseph C. Winter. It is available from the University of Oklahoma Press. www.oupress.com, or write them at 2600 Venture Dr., Norman, OK 73069. Tel. 405-325-2000.

Photo Richard Pocker ©

Nicotiana rustica toppled from the weight of the seedpods. Growers of
tobacco leaf would usually top the plant (remove the flowers) to encourage
more leaf growth. This plant was started from seeds over
one hundred years old.

Among the stranger proposed uses for tobacco plants was to utilize the plant as a mine detector.

The Geneva-based International Campaign to Ban Landmines claims there are an average of 15,000–20,000 deaths annually when innocent victims come in contact with the left over devices from wars that raged in Angola, Cambodia, Sudan, Afghanistan, Bosnia, and many other countries. It is estimated there are over 100 million mines spread out over 77,000 square miles.

Mine detection is a slow, risky process. Metal detectors have hundreds of false readings when sweeping for mines. It also requires a risky close proximity to the mine, putting the operator in danger.

In 2004, a Danish company experimented with a genetically modified tobacco plant. They claimed the flower would turn red in the presence of nitrogen dioxide, a chemical given off by explosives.

In theory, a field could be sprayed with a hydroseeder, such as is used to grow grass at a golf course, but in this case, the spray would contain the seeds of the modified tobacco. Wherever the plant was in the proximity of a landmine, the red tobacco flowers would flag the spot.

In addition, being a genetically modified plant, the new seeds it produced would be sterile, and the field could be reverted to agriculture or another use.

Testing went on for a few years at military-ordnance fields. But by 2008, they gave up.

That is too bad. They only tried one type of tobacco for the test.

To paraphrase Thomas Edison, he said he had to find out thousands of things that were not suitable to make a lightbulb filament before he stumbled on tungsten.

Perhaps they gave up too soon.

SHIRAZI

Photo: Adaptive Seeds © **Shirazi Tobacco Flower**

Common Name: Shirazi Tobacco

What Orinoco tobacco was to Virginia, the founding of America, and the formation of the American Revolution, Shirazi was to Iran.

Shirazi is a unique Oriental tobacco, used as a blending tobacco because of its strong flavor. In the late nineteenth century, Iran was thrust into mass protests over the attempts of a British monopoly to control the market. It was the first successful protest against British interference in Iran.

For our gardens, it has a unique white blossom with a lavender tinge. It grows in a columnar fashion of light-green leaves. It is about 48 inches high with leaves about 24 inches long. The leaves end in a cup, which gives the appearance of a beak. It is very suitable for medium or large containers. In the garden, space them about 16–20 inches apart. Shirazi tolerates a wide range of soils, but regular fertilizing will be required for the best results.

Photo: Adaptive Seeds © **Shirazi Tobacco**

Sources:
Daggawalla
Adaptive Seeds
Virginia Tobacco Seeds, Spain
Allies
Northwood Seeds
New Hope
Sustainable Seeds
Adaptive Seeds
Heirloom Tobacco

SHIREY

Photo: Westseed Farm © **Shirey Tobacco Flower**

Common Name: Shirey

This heirloom is classified as a "dark" tobacco; the leaves when cured turn a dark or medium brown. Commercial tobacco farmers raise this variety for its bold flavor. There are sources that sell smaller quantities of seed for our use.

In the garden, Shirey puts forth a beautiful, pinkish-red cluster of flowers with a large leaf. It grows to about 60 inches high and matures in sixty-five days. Plant Shirey in loose loam and full to partial sun. It does not require frequent watering.

Photo: northwoodseeds.com © **Shirey Tobacco**

Sources:
Northwood Seeds
JL Hudson
B&T
The Tobacco Seed Co., UK
Sustainable Seeds
Virginia Tobacco Seeds, Spain
West Seed Farm

SILK LEAF

Photo: northwoodseeds.com © **Silk Leaf Tobacco**

Common Name: Silk Leaf Tobacco

In the 1940s, this heirloom was a popular heirloom variety among commercial farmers. It has fallen out of favor, and the seeds are rare. Characteristic of "brightleaf" tobacco, Silk Leaf yellows from the bottom up as the plant matures. It will give an "Old Virginia" character to your garden. In addition to its clusters of pink flowers, it grows to about 72 inches high with an abundance of leaves that are about 20 inches long and 12 inches wide.

Space them about 12–16 inches apart in loose loam, full sun, and they need frequent watering.

Sources:
Northwood Seeds
New Hope
Sustainable Seeds
West Seed Farm

SMALL STALK BLACK MAMMOTH

Photo: Daggawalla Seeds ©
Small Stalk Black Mammoth Tobacco Flower

Common Name: Small Stalk Black Mammoth

This heirloom is prized by commercial growers for its deep, dark-brown color when cured, Small Stalk Black Mammoth, because of its large-size leaves, is used for cigar wrappers.

The plants are smaller than other Mammoth varieties, reaching a peak of 36 inches high. Grow it for the abundance of leaves. It is excellent container plant both indoors and out.
In the garden, space them 18–24 inches apart in full sun and loose loam. This plant requires frequent watering.

Photo: northwoodseeds.com © **Small Stalk Black Mammoth Tobacco**

Sources:
Northwood Seeds
Daggawalla
JL Hudson
Sustainable Seeds
Virginia Tobacco Seeds, Spain

SOUTHERN BEAUTY

Photo: Sustainable Seeds © **Southern Beauty Tobacco**

Common Name: Southern Beauty

With gorgeous, wide-mouth pink and white flowers, I would like to think this nicotiana derived its name from them. But in the world of tobacco farming, most likely the large columnar leaves were the reason.

Southern Beauty grows to over 72 inches high in less than fifty-five days with leaves that exceed 30 inches long and 24 inches wide. It requires full sun and regular fertilizing for best results.

Sources:
New Hope
Northwood Seeds
Sustainable Seeds
The Tobacco Seed Co., UK
West Seed Farm

STAG HORN

Photo: *northwoodseeds.com* © **Stag Horn Tobacco**

Common Name: Stag Horn Tobacco

Stag Horn is an heirloom "dark" Virginia tobacco. Dark is the label for tobaccos that cure to a dark-brown or reddish color.

It derives its name from the curl at the end of long, narrow leaves that resembles a horn.

Growing to nearly 72 inches high, it matures in about sixty-five days. Space them about 20 inches apart in loose loam and full sun.

Sources:
Northwood Seeds
The Tobacco Seed Co., UK
Sustainable Seeds

SUAVEOLENS

Suaveolens Tobacco Flower

Common Name: Australian Tobacco

Binominal Name: nicotiana suaveolens

Synonyms: nicotiana undulata; nicotiana exigua

A native nicotiana found in the coastal areas of New South Wales and Victoria, Australia. The plants grow from four to six feet tall on thin, branching stalks. The flowers are white with a slight red tinge. They are found on rocky and sandy soil.

There are several native nicotiana found throughout Australia. Seed sources are difficult to find, but suaveolens is one type that can be found from time to time.

More information about native plants in Australia is available on-line from the Royal Botanic Garden in Sydney, Australia, at their website—rbgsyd.nsw.gov.au.

Photo by permission of Colleen Miller ©
Suaveolens in New South Wales Australia

Sources:
De Werkplaats, Netherlands
Seedman.com (UK only)
Thompson & Morgan, UK & US

SYLVESTRIS

Photo: Richard Pocker © **Sylvestris Tobacco Flower**

Common Names: Sylvestris; Argentine Tobacco; Woodland Tobacco; South American tobacco; Only the Lonely

Binominal Name: Nicotiana tabacum sylvestris

Stunning clusters of white drooping flowers form on a central spike. They are about 3.5 inches long with flaring tubes about 2 inches across. They are very sweet scented and will perfume the air on warm summer nights. The plants grow to about 60 inches tall with large-textured, ovate-shaped leaves with a slightly wavy edge. The leaves grow to about 12 inches long.

Sylvestris is thick-stemmed and a good choice in windy locations. The leaves decrease in size up the stem giving the plant stability under most conditions.

It is a good beginner's plant, easy to start and grow. It is also an excellent choice for indoors. In warm locations, seeds will fall and winter-over for the following spring.

Plant about 16 inches apart in well-drained soil and in full sun to partial shade.

*Photo: Richard Pocker © **Sylvestris Tobacco***

Sources:
Allies
Diane's Seeds
King Seeds NZ
New Hope

Plant World Seeds, UK
Sarah Raven, UK
Seedaholic
Special Plants, UK
The Tobacco Seed Co., UK
Seeds of Eaden
Terroir Seeds
B&T
D T Brown, UK
Hardy Plants
JL Hudson
Nicky's, UK
Portland Nursery (plants only)
Silene, Belgium
Swallowtail
Sustainable Seeds
Terroir Seeds
The Flower Company
Thompson & Morgan, UK & US
Select Seeds
White Flower Farms (plants only)
Nuts n Cones, UK
Von Trapp Greenhouse (plants only)
Northwood Seeds
Chiltern, UK
Impecta, Sweden
Botanical Interests
Seedman.com

TREE

Photo: Cibergarden © **Tree Tobacco Flower**

Tree tobacco deviates from the usual run of tobacco species. It is a conspicuous evergreen, loosely branching shrub, six to fifteen feet tall, becoming a small tree at times up to twenty feet. It seems much at home on the desert as near the coast. Its slender, graceful branches are generously supplied with handsome blue-green foliage, both leaves and stems quite hairless...It originated in Argentina and came to us by way of Mexico during the Mission period, brought along to make a new environment more home-like, having quite a vogue in early California gardens.[4]

Common Names: Tree Tobacco; Glauca; Brazilian Tree; San Juan Tree; Mexican Tree;

Blue Tree; Mustard Tree

Binominal Name: Nicotiana glauca

---

[4] Mary Beal, *Desert Magazine*, August (1944): 2–3

This variety of nicotiana will do fine in a medium to large planter. It will grow to about 72 inches in a planter as in the photo below. The leaves have thin stems and trumpet-shaped yellow flowers that are wonderful hummingbird attractors. In warmer climates, it is a perennial that can grow to 20 feet tall.

Photo: Richard Pocker © **Tree Tobacco**

Sources:
The Tobacco Seed Co., UK
B&T
Chiltern, UK
Daggawalla
Heirloom Tobacco
JL Hudson
Virginia Tobacco Seeds, Spain

VIRGINIA

Photo: Beth B. Pocker © **Virginia 309 Flower**

Common Names: Virginia; Virginia Brightleaf; Virginia Gold; Virginia Smoking: Virginia Cigarette

Virginia is a "brightleaf" tobacco (see **Silk Leaf** for explanation) that was believed to be originally from Guatemala. It is possibly the strain that supplanted Orinoco (see **Orinoco**) in the Virginia colonies. Brightleaf is commonly known as Virginia tobacco regardless of where it comes from.

What they have in common is a mild flavor and low nicotine content, large foliage, clusters of pink flowers, and the leaves cure to a light yellow. It grows from 36 to 48 inches tall. Plant about 20 inches apart in loose loam and full sun. Virginia-type tobaccos require regular fertilizing.

Photo: northwoodseeds.com © **Virginia 509 Tobacco**

Sources:
Virginia-Heirloom Tobacco
Virginia-Impecta, Sweden`
Virginia 116-Northwood Seeds
Virginia 116-Sustainable Seeds
Virginia Bright-Victory Seeds
Virginia Bright Leaf-New Hope
Virginia Gold-Cibergarden, Spain

Virginia Gold-Daggawalla
Virginia Gold-The Tobacco Seed Co., UK
Virginia Gold-Virginia Tobacco Seeds, Spain
Virginia Spanish-Virginia Tobacco Seeds, Spain
Virginia VA 309-JL Hudson
Virginia VA 309-B&T
Virginia VA 509-Sustainable Seeds

VUELTA ABAJO

Photo: northwoodseeds.com © **Vuelta Abajo Tobacco Leaf**

Common Name: Vuelta Abajo; Vuelta

Binominal Name: nicotiana tabacum vuelta abajo

This heirloom variety is considered the finest of the Cuban tobaccos. Named after the providence in the extreme western part of Cuba, the name refers to any tobacco coming from that area.

Classified as an "Oriental" tobacco because of its strong flavor and high nicotine content, the plants grow in a pyramid shape topped with pink flowers. Plants are about 48 inches high. The leaves are generally 12 to 15 inches long and 8 to 10 inches wide. Plant in loose loam, full sun, and water frequently.

Photo: northwoodseeds.com © **Vuelta Abajo Tobacco**

Sources:
Heirloom Tobacco
Northwood Seeds
Sustainable Seeds

WALKER'S BROADLEAF

Photo: northwoodseeds.com © **Walker's Broadleaf Tobacco**

Common Name: Walker's Broadleaf

Walker's Broadleaf is an heirloom that may have been developed from a strain of Maryland Broadleaf tobacco back in the 1880s. Its true history is lost.

Walker's Broadleaf grows to about 72 inches high with leaves that are 20–24 inches long and 12 to 16 inches wide. Topped with clusters of pink flowers, the leaves on the plant turn light green and mottled when ripe. Matures in fifty-five to sixty days.

Space them 12–16 inches apart in loose loam and full sun.

Sources:
Northwood Seeds
JL Hudson
B&T
Sustainable Seeds

YELLOW PRIOR

Photo: Westseed Farm © **Yellow Prior Tobacco**

Common Name: Yellow Prior

Yellow Prior is an heirloom "brightleaf" tobacco that is first listed in a catalogue in 1884. Brightleaf tobaccos date back to just after the War of 1812 when a new, lighter variety began to replace the dark, flu-cured types in America.

It is a 48-inch, columnar plant on sturdy stalks, topped with pink flowers. The leaves tend to stand upright as in the photo. Plant them 12–16 inches apart in loose loam and full sun.

Sources:
New Hope
Northwood Seeds
The Tobacco Seed Co., UK
West Seed Farm
Sustainable Seeds

YENIDJE

Photo: Richard Pocker ©

Yenidje Tobacco. Note the extreme sucker running off the left side of the stem. Normally, it would have been snapped off as soon as it appeared. Suckers can sap the strength of the plant, causing stunted growth and smaller leaves.

Tobacco is cultivated all over Turkey, but the production is not the same everywhere. There are four varieties, the Bafra, the Mannisea, the Yenidje and the Djabel…the Yenidje, which is a production of European Turkey, is, by reason of climate and soil, of a quality not equaled anywhere in the world.[5]
Frank Leslie's Popular Monthly, 1886

---

[5] *Frank Leslie's Popular Monthly* 22 (1886): 655

Common Name: Yenidje

This heirloom variety dates back from a strain that originated in ancient Macedonia. Many modified types were developed from this pure type. It was and still is raised in a small production setting. Demand often outstrips supply.

What we have is a charming columnar plant topped with pink flowers, small leaves and a history that leaves us at a doorway to our path of the glory of Western Civilization.

Yenidje grows to about 36 inches high. It has small leaves that are about 7 to 12 inches long. Plant Yenidje 12–16 inches apart in full sun. It tolerates many types of soil from loose loam to sandy.

Sources:
Heirloom Tobacco
Northwood Seeds
Sustainable Seeds

YUMBO

Photo: northwoodseeds.com © **Yumbo Tobacco**

Common Name: Yumbo

Yumbo originates from the Amazonian tribe of that name. They reside in the upper Amazon basin of Columbia. **It is a sacred tobacco, high in alkaloids, and the leaves should be handled with extreme caution.**

Growing to 30 inches high with thick, dark-green leaves and pink flowers, it is a fast grower and matures in fifty days. Plant them 12–16 inches apart in loose loam to sandy soil and full sun.

Sources:
Heirloom Tobacco
Northwood Seeds
Sustainable Seeds

ZIMMER SPANISH

Zimmer Spanish Tobacco

Common Name: Zimmer Spanish; Zimmer

Developed shortly after the Civil War, Zimmer Spanish came from a strain of Havana and was developed and grown in the Miami Valley area of Ohio. It was named after a prominent tobacco grower in the valley.

Growing to a height of 48 inches, the leaves are dense and are set close together and topped with pink flowers. Plant them 16–20 inches apart in full sun and loose loam.

Sources:
New Hope
West Seed Farm

Chapter 5

NURSERY HYBRID TOBACCO

An Introduction

Several garden series of nicotianas have been developed from N. alata that are much more compact and hold their flowers better, but don't have the fragrance of the original species. The semi-dwarf "Nicki" series is only 16 to 18 inches tall and produces red, white, rose, or lime-green flowers. In 1979, "Nicki Red" was the first nicotiana to win an All-America Selections® award and offered gardeners shorter, uniform height and good weather tolerance in addition to flowers that bloomed from spring to fall.

Even shorter is the "Saratoga" series, which features compact plants only 10 to 12 inches tall. "Saratoga" blooms early, has a light evening scent, and is available in seven different colors and two mixtures, including lime-green, deep-rose, white, pink, and a purple bicolor.

The intriguing "Tinkerbell" (Nicotiana x hybrida) is another ornamental tobacco that appeals to the gardener looking for something very different. The dusky rose petals face outward from long, green trumpets for a unique color combination. In the center of each flower is the remarkable blue pollen. The medium-sized plants grow to 3 feet and bloom throughout the summer.

Many of the new garden hybrids come from the group Nicotiana x sanderae, including the 2006 All-America

*Selections® Award-winning Nicotiana "Perfume Deep Purple."
The beautiful, 2-inch long, deep purple flowers hold their col-
or well and give off a nice, light fragrance in the evening. In
addition, plants are easy to maintain for beautiful blooms all
summer, even through heat. No pinching, deadheading or prun-
ing is required to keep plants neat and attractive. This medium
sized plant reaches about 20 inches tall and up to 18 inches
wide. There are other spectacular colors in the "Perfume" series,
including a stunning lilac-blue flower and "Antique Lime,"
featuring a tan reverse on the back of the star-shaped flower.*

*The "Domino" series is an intermediate sized nicotiana avail-
able in 13 colors with upward facing flowers in red, white, crim-
son-pink, lime-green, and bicolors with white-center eyes or colored
margins. Plants bloom early, have a nice form, and reach a mature
height of 12 to 18 inches.*

*"Avalon Bright Pink" nicotiana won both the 2001 All-
America Selections® award and the European Fleuroselect Gold
Medal for its attractive bright pastel pink flowers that stand out in
the garden. The very dwarf plants reach a mature height of only 10
inches and spread up to 12 inches making them ideal for borders
and containers. Among the other colors in the Avalon series are a
unique lime-green and purple-bicolor, as well as a charming white
and pink-picotee.*

*The always-popular "Sensation Mix" is a dependable variety
with fragrant flowers in shades of pink, red, and white that stay
open all day into the evening. Taller than many of the hybrids, this
variety reaches 2.5 to 3 feet tall.*

National Garden Bureau—2009 Year of the Nicotiana

Unlike commercial tobacco, where the hybrids are developed for the leaf yield, flavor, maturation time, and disease resistance, the garden-variety hybrids are at the whim
of fashion.

With a more extensive color selection and compact size, nursery hybrids will make you into a tobacco famer with aplomb.

Seeds for some varieties may be a challenge to find, but more and more garden centers are carrying these annual nocitiana varieties as bedder plants.

AVALON

Photo: National Garden Bureau ©
Avalon Mixed Tobacco

Common Names: AVALON: Appleblossom; Bright Pink; Burgundy; Lime; Lime & Purple; Mixed Dwarf; Peach; Pink Picotee; Red; Salmon; White

Binominal Name: Nicotiana X sanderae f1 avalon

This is a series of evening-scented, tubular, five-star flowers that are available in white, pink, light pink, lime-green, violet, and plum. They do well in planters and as borders in full sun to light shade. The plants are bushy with dark-green leaves. They grow to about 12 inches high. Space them 12–16 inches apart. Although this is a hybrid, it might overwinter for one season in warmer climates.

The clusters of flowers last from July to September with little care beyond regular watering. Their increasing popularity means they are now found at nurseries as bedder plants as well as seeds.

Sources:
Avalon Appleblossom-B&T
Avalon Appleblossom-Hazzard's Seed Store
Avalon Appleblossom-Impecta, Sweden
Avalon Appleblossom-Moles Seeds, UK
Avalon Appleblossom-Nuts n Cones, UK
Avalon Appleblossom-Pase Seeds
Avalon Appleblosson-Seed Tapestry
Avalon Bright Pink-Dobies, UK
Avalon Bright Pink-Seed Tapestry
Avalon Burgundy-Hazzard's Seed Store
Avalon Burgundy-Pase Seeds
Avalon Burgundy-Seed Tapestry
Avalon Lime-B&T
Avalon Lime-Hazzard's Seed Store
Avalon Lime-Moles Seeds, UK
Avalon Lime-Nuts n Cones, UK
Avalon Lime-Pase Seeds
Avalon Lime-Purple Bicolor-Nuts n Cones, UK
Avalon Lime-Purple Bicolor-Hazzard's Seed Store
Avalon Lime-Purple Bicolor-Summer Hill
Avalon Mixed-D T Brown, UK
Avalon Mixed-Harris Seeds
Avalon Mixed-Hazzard's Seed Store
Avalon Mixed-Nut n Cones, UK
Avalon Mixed-Swallowtail
Avalon Mixed Dwarf-B&T
Avalon Peach-Seed Tapestry
Avalon Picotee-Impecta, Sweden
Avalon Pink Picotee-B&T

Avalon Pink Picotee-Nuts n Cones, UK
Avalon Pink Picotee-Seed Tapestry
Avalon Pink Picotee-Summer Hill
Avalon Red-B&T
Avalon Red-Hazzard's Seed Store
Avalon Red-Nuts n Cones, UK
Avalon Red-Pase Seeds
Avalon Red-Seed Tapestry
Avalon White-B&T
Avalon White-Hazzard's Seed Store
Avalon White-Impecta, Sweden
Avalon White-Nuts n Cones, UK
Avalon White-Pase Seeds
Avalon White-Seed Tapestry

BABYBELLA

Photo: Rob Broekhuis www.robsplants.com © **Babybella Tobacco**

Common Name: Babybella or Baby Bella

Binominal Name: Nicotiana X sanderae f1 babybella

Babybella is a mass of wine-red tubular flowers on 36-inch stems. It is more compact that the similar, Tinkerbell, and is highly suitable for container planting as a result. It blooms from July to September. Space 12–16 inches apart in loose loam to sandy soil. It is best in full sun but can tolerate partial shade.

Sources:
Robs Plants, UK
Hazzard's Seeds
Nicky's Nursery, UK

Park Seeds
Summer Hill Seeds
Swallowtail Seeds
Von Trapp (bedder plants only)

BLACK KNIGHT

Photo: Silene.be © **Black Knight Tobacco**

Common Name: Black Knight

Binominal Name: Nicotiana X sanderae f1 black knight

Black Night is similar to Tinkerbell but with darker red tubular flowers. Heavy blooming on tall stalks 48–60 inches high. Blooms last July to September. Space them 12–16 inches apart in well-drained loam or sandy soil. Black Knight prefers full sun but will tolerate partial shade.

Sources:
De Werkplaats, Netherlands
Sarah Raven, UK
Silene, Belgium

DOMINO

Photo: Richard Pocker ©
Domino Lime Tobacco

Common Names: DOMINO: Antique Peach; Antique Red; Antique Shades; Crimson; Light Purple; Lime Green; Mixed; Pink White Eye; Purple; Purple White Eye; Rose Picotee; Salmon Pink; White.

Binominal Name: Nicotiana X sanderae f1 domino

This compact variety of nicotiana has a high tolerance for heat and humidity. They are sweet scented with vast clusters of star-shaped flowers with dark-green foliage. Excellent growers in container and one of the best for scented hanging baskets. The plants grow 12–16 inches high.

Again, as colors go in and out of fashion, it will take some searching or waiting for certain color varieties to return to availability.

Sources:
Domino-Portland Nursery (plants only)
Domino-Antique Shades-Nicky's, UK
Domino Mixed-Dobies, UK
Domino Mixed-Hazzard's Seed Store
Domino Mixed-HPS
Domino Mixed-Richbar (plants only)
Domino Salmon Pink-Hazzard's Seed Store
Domino Salmon Pink-Summer Hill
Domino Salmon Pink-Von Trapp Greenhouse (plants only)
Domino White-Hazzard's Seed Store

DWARF WHITE BEDDER

Photo: Wikimedia.org **Dwarf White Bedder Tobacco**

Common Name: Dwarf White Bedder

Binominal Name: Nicotiana X sanderae f1 dwarf white bedder

Although this stunning white flowered dwarf nicotiana is not currently available, it is worth watching for in the event a breeder brings it back. There are no current sources.

Dwarf White Bedder stands about 18 inches high, but it is one of the more scented plants in this size category. It has thin branching stems and has a bushy appearance.

FRAGRANT CLOUD

Photo: plant-seed-world.com © **Fragrant Cloud Tobacco**

Common Name: Fragrant Cloud

Binominal Name: Nicotiana X sanderae f1 fragrant cloud

This is the tall, thin cousin to Dwarf White Bedder with its large, white flowers on stalks that reach up to 36 inches high. The leaves are dark green. From July to September, they will give off a night-time fragrance. Plant them close to your house or in tubs in sunny locations. In the garden, space them 12–16 inches apart in full sun to partial shade.

Source:
Plant World Seeds, UK
Thompson & Morgan

Spring Hill
Hazzard's
Daggawalla
Seedman.com

HAVANA HYBRID

Photo: Wikimedia; Henryk Zychowski **Havana Red Hybrid Tobacco**

Common Names: HAVANA: Appleblossom; Carmine Rose; Lilac Rose; Lime; Mixed; Purple; Red; True Lime; White.

Binominal Name: Nicotiana X sanderae f1 havana

The Havana series is a very compact hybrid for borders and containers. It does not have a scent. Its popularity may be waning, and there are few sources for the seeds, but bedder plants may be available at local nurseries.

Thin stems and they stand about 18 inches high. Space them 12–16 inches apart in the garden. They need full sun and well-drained soil.

Sources:
Nicky's Nursery, UK-Appleblossom
Richbar Nursery-Carmine Red or Rose
Hardy Plants-Lilac Rose

HOT CHOCOLATE

Photo: Special Plants, UK © **Hot Chocolate Tobacco**

Common Name: Hot Chocolate

Binominal Name: X sanderae f1 hot chocolate

A hybrid developed from a strain of nicotiana langsdorfii, the tall, multibranching stems end in tubular flowers that are dark mauve to chocolate in color. The color is more robust if the plants are in sunny areas. It grows to 36 to 48 inches tall. It gives more saturated colors when given full sun. Space the plants 12–16 inches apart in well-drained loam or sandy soil.

A plant that is so unusual it will become a focal point of the garden. It also thrives in large planters.

Sources:
Special Plants, UK
Nicky's, UK

B&T Seeds
Annie's
The Flower Company (bedding plants only)
Terrapin Gardens (bedding plants only)

NICKI

Photo: All American Selection © **Nicki Red Tobacco**

Common Names: Nicki; Lime; Mixed; Red; Rose; White

Binominal Name: Nicotiana X sanderae f1 nicki

Nicki Red was named the All-American Selection Award winner in 1979. It maintains a low-dwarf form, staying under 18 inches high at maturity, with crowds of solid color flowers. The leaves are bright green and covered with short, sticky hairs. Nicki thrives in full sun but will tolerate partial shade. Plant them 12–16 inches apart in loose loam or sandy soil. They are excellent container plants.

Sources:
Nicki Lime-Chiltern, UK
Nicki Mixed-Chiltern, UK
Nicki Mixed-Nuts n Cones, UK
Nicki Rose-Chiltern, UK
Nicki White-Chiltern, UK

PERFUME

Photo: Special Plants, UK © **Perfume Purple Tobacco**

Common Names: PERFUME: Antique Lime Blue; Bright Rose; Lime; Mixed; Purple; Red; White.

Binominal Name: Nicotiana X sanderae f1 perfume

The Perfume series is of the most popular of the hybrid nursery nicotiana. It was a 2006 All-American Selection winner. Highly fragrant, they last for days as cut flowers. The plants have drifts of two inches, star-shaped flowers on compact stems. They grow to 12 to 16 inches high. Easy to grow, they are a good beginner plant and attract butterflies and bees with their fragrance. They are an excellent container or border plant. The Perfume series are high-heat tolerant. Space them 12–16 inches apart in well-drained loam or sandy soil.

Sources:
Perfume Antique Lime-Nuts n Cones, UK
Perfume Antique Lime-Seed Tapestry

Perfume Antique Lime-Silene, Belgium
Perfume Antique Lime-Swallowtail
Perfume Blue-Glacier Gardens (plants only)
Perfume Blue-Hazzard's Seed Store
Perfume Blue-Nuts n Cones, UK
Perfume Blue-Seed Tapestry
Perfume Blue-Silene, Belgium
Perfume Blue-Summer Hill
Perfume Bright Rose-Hazzard's Seed Store
Perfume Bright Rose-Nuts n Cones, UK
Perfume Bright Rose-Seed Tapestry
Perfume Deep Purple-Hardy Plants
Perfume Deep Purple-Hazzard's Seed Store
Perfume Deep Purple-HPS
Perfume Deep Purple-Nuts n Cones, UK
Perfume Deep Purple-Park Seeds
Perfume Deep Purple-Seed Tapestry
Perfume Deep Purple-Select Seeds
Perfume Deep Purple-Swallowtail
Perfume Deep Purple-Thompson & Morgan, US & UK
Perfume Lilac-Seed Tapestry
Perfume Lime-Hazzard's Seed Store
Perfume Lime-Summer Hill
Perfume Lime Green-Von Trapp Greenhouse (plants only)
Perfume Mixed-D T Brown, UK
Perfume Mixed-Hardy Plants
Perfume Mixed-Harris Seeds
Perfume Mixed-Hazzard's Seed Store
Perfume Mixed-J. W. Jung
Perfume Mixed-Nicky's, UK only
Perfume Mixed-Nuts n Cones, UK
Perfume Mixed-Park Seeds
Perfume Mixed-Seed Tapestry
Perfume Mixed-Suttons Seeds, UK
Perfume Mixed-Swallowtail

Perfume Mixed-Von Trapp Greenhouse (plants only)
Perfume Purple-Sarah Raven, UK
Perfume Purple-Silene, Belgium
Perfume Purple-Special Plants, UK
Perfume Red-Hazzard's Seed Store
Perfume Red-Nuts n Cones, UK
Perfume Red-Seed Tapestry
Perfume Red-Silene, Belgium
Perfume Red-Summer Hill
Perfume White -Hazzard's Seed Store
Perfume White-Nuts n Cones, UK
Perfume White-Seed Tapestry
Perfume White-Silene, Belgium
Perfume White-Swallowtail

SARATOGA

Photo: National Garden Bureau © **Saratoga Mixed Tobacco**

Common Names: SARATOGA: Antique Shades; Appleblossom; Deep Rose; Lime; Mixed; Pink; Purple Bicolored; Red; Rose; White.

Binominal Name: Nicotiana X sanderae f1 saratoga

One of the most popular nursery hybrids, the Saratoga series is unique among the nicotiana as it thrives in either full sun or shade. It is fragrant in late afternoon and early evening. Saratoga is very compact. The leaves are oblong rosettes at the base. It rarely exceeds 12 inches in height. It is an excellent container plant or a border accent.

Sources:
Saratoga Antique Shades-Seed Tapestry
Saratoga Appleblossom-Glacier Gardens (plants only)
Saratoga Appleblossom-Hardy Plants
Saratoga Appleblossom-Hazzard's Seed Store
Saratoga Appleblossom-Seed Tapestry
Saratoga Bicolor-Seed Tapestry
Saratoga Deep Rose-Glacier Gardens (plants only)
Saratoga Deep Rose-Richbar (plants only)
Saratoga Deep Rose-Seed Tapestry
Saratoga Deep Rose-Wasco (plants only)
Saratoga Lime-B&T
Saratoga Lime-Hazzard's Seed Store
Saratoga Lime-Richbar (plants only)
Saratoga Lime-Seed Tapestry
Saratoga Mixed-Hart's (plants only)
Saratoga Mixed-Hazzard's Seed Store
Saratoga Mixed-Seed Tapestry
Saratoga Mixed-Wasco (plants only)
Saratoga Purple-Seed Tapestry
Saratoga Purple Bicolor-Hart's (plants only)
Saratoga Purple Bicolor-Hazzard's Seed Store
Saratoga Red-Hart's (plants only)
Saratoga Red-Richbar (plants only)
Saratoga Red-Seed Tapestry
Saratoga Red Assorted-Glacier Gardens (plants only)
Saratoga Rose-Seed Tapestry
Saratoga White-Hart's (plants only)
Saratoga White-Seed Tapestry
Saratoga White-Wasco (plants only)

STARMAKER

Photo: Beth B. Pocker ©

Starmaker Appleblossom

Photo: Beth B. Pocker © **Starmaker Deep Lime Tobacco**

Common Names: Starmaker; Appleblossom; Burgundy; Cherry Blossom; Lilac; Mixed; Pink; Red; Rose Pink; White

Binominal Name: Nicotiana X sanderae f1 starmaker

Formerly known as Starship, the name has changed but not the sensational colors. It grows to about 18 inches high. It has thin stems with dark-green, ovate-shaped leaves. Plant them about 12 inches apart in loose loam or sandy soil. It tolerates full sun or partial shade.

Sources:
No current seed sources but frequently found as bedder plants at local nurseries.

TINKERBELL

Photo: plant-world-seeds.com © **Tinkerbell Tobacco Flower**

Common Name: Tinkerbell

Binominal Name: Nicotiana X sanderae f1 tinkerbell

This is a hybrid that I find exciting to grow. Tinkerbell is a heavy blooming on long stalks. They grow to about 30 inches high. The flowers are long, green trumpets ending in a dusky red petal with unique blue pollen centers. Although similar in appearance to Babybella, they are taller. Plant in full sun or partial shade in loose loam to sandy soil.

Photo: National Garden Bureau © **Tinkerbell Tobacco**

Sources:
B&T
De Werkplaats, Netherlands
Nuts n Cones, UK
Portland Nursery (plants only)
Silene, Belgium
Special Plants, UK
Swallowtail

WHISPER

Photo: Richard Pocker © **Whisper Mixed Tobacco**

Common Name: Whisper Mixed

Binominal Name: Nicotiana X sanderae f1 whisper

One of the taller nursery hybrids, Whisper is a fragrant, showy plant for the back of the border. The basal, light-green leaves and stems end in hundreds of small flowers that open red in color but soon fade to shades of pink and white, giving a tricolor appearance.

They grow to 36 inches high and they do best in full sun. Space them about 16 inches apart in the garden in loose loam to sandy soil.

Whisper has a delicious evening fragrance and is a wonderful plant for cut flowers.

Sources:
Thompson & Morgan
Sarah Raven, UK
Mr. Fothergill's, UK
Silene
Seeds of Eaden, UK

C h a p t e r   6

DISEASES AND PESTS OF TOBACCO

D iseases and pests cause major losses to commercial tobacco farmers every year. The disease pathogens fall into several categories: fungi, bacteria, viruses, nematodes, mycoplasmas, and other parasitic invaders.

The name most commonly recognized is tobacco mosaic virus, which is also a common problem of tomato plants. Fungi problems such as Blue Mold, Powdery Mildew, and Brown Spot are among the most common of the leaf diseases. Fungi can attack the roots and result in Black Shank, Black Root Rot, Stem Rot, or Sore Shin among others.

Most viruses are harmful to tobacco plants, but some can be beneficial to the tobacco flower. Nursery hybrid flowers can have color breaks, creating an interesting pattern in the petals, caused by Mild Green Mosaic Virus. It works in the same ways that color breaks became the rage of Dutch tulips in the seventeenth century.

It is beyond the scope of this book to delve into the details of the dozens of diseases that affect commercial growers. The vast types of commercial hybrid tobaccos are cultivated to deal with the propensities of particular varieties and provide certain immunity to specific ills.

Insects such as Japanese beetles can be removed by hand. Aphids can be washed off with insecticidal soaps.

When growing tobacco for **ornamental purposes,** I have found commercial fungicides and insecticides to be effective. **Again, I remind the reader that the purpose of this book is to introduce** flowering nicotiana for ornamental gardens. Do not plan to use the leaf for any purpose if you use commercial insecticides or fungicides. Please use common sense.

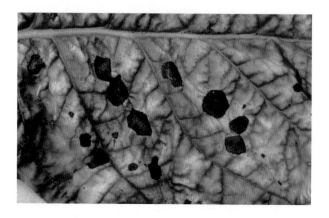

Photo: R.J. Reynolds Tobacco Company Slide Set, R.J. Reynolds Tobacco Company, Bugwood.org

Brown Spot

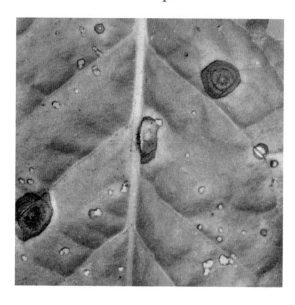

Photo: Clemson University-USDA Cooperative Extension Slide Series, Bugwood.org

Frog-Eye Leafspot

Photo: R.J. Reynolds Tobacco Company Slide Set, R.J.
Reynolds Tobacco Company, Bugwood.org
Tobacco Hornworm

Photo: R.J. Reynolds Tobacco Company Slide Set, R.J.
Reynolds Tobacco Company, Bugwood.org
Tobacco Hornworm Moth

Photo: Clemson University-USDA Cooperative Extension Slide Series, Bugwood.org

Tobacco Aphids

Photo: R.J. Reynolds Tobacco Company Slide Set, R.J. Reynolds Tobacco Company, Bugwood.org

Grasshopper Damage

*Photo: R.J. Reynolds Tobacco Company Slide Set, R.J.
Reynolds Tobacco Company, Bugwood.org*
Blue Mold

*Photo: R.J. Reynolds Tobacco Company Slide Set, R.J.
Reynolds Tobacco Company, Bugwood.org*
Japanese Beetle Damage

Photo: R.J. Reynolds Tobacco Company Slide Set, R.J.
Reynolds Tobacco Company, Bugwood.org
Tobacco Etch Virus

Photo: R.J. Reynolds Tobacco Company Slide Set, R.J.
Reynolds Tobacco Company, Bugwood.org
Tobacco Mosaic Virus

Photo: R.J. Reynolds Tobacco Company Slide Set, R.J. Reynolds Tobacco Company, Bugwood.org

Black Root Rot

Photo:, UKY.org

Black Shank

Diseases of Tobacco

Foliar Diseases Caused by Fungi

- ☐ Blue Mold
- ☐ Powdery Mildwew
- ☐ Brown Spot
- ☐ Anthracnose
- ☐ Frogeye
- ☐ Target Spot
- ☐ Gray Mold
- ☐ Ragged Leaf Spot
- ☐ Phyllosticta Leaf Spot
- ☐ Corynespora Leaf Spot
- ☐ Curvularia Leaf Spot
- ☐ Scab
- ☐ Rust

Root and Stem Diseases Caused by Fungi

- ☐ Black Shank
- ☐ Pythium Diseases
- ☐ Black Root Rot
- ☐ Stem Rot
- ☐ Sore Shin and Damping-Off
- ☐ Fusarium Wilt
- ☐ Verticillium Wilt
- ☐ Charcoal Rot
- ☐ Tobacco Stunt
- ☐ Olpidium Seedling Blight
- ☐ Collar Rot

Foliar Diseases Caused by Bacteria

- ❑ Wildfire and Angular Leaf Spot
- ❑ Hollow Stalk
- ❑ Black Leg
- ❑ Barn Rot
- ❑ Philippine Bacterial Leaf Spot
- ❑ Leafy Gall

Root Diseases Caused by Bacteria

- ❑ Bacterial Wilt

Diseases Caused by Mycoplasma-Like Organisms

- ❑ Aster Yellows
- ❑ Stolbur
- ❑ Big Bud

Diseases Caused by Nematodes

- ❑ Root-Knot Nematodes
- ❑ Tobacco Cyst Nematodes
- ❑ Lesions Nematodes
- ❑ Stem Nematodes
- ❑ Ectoparasitic Nematodes

Diseases Caused by Viruses

- ❑ Tobacco Mosaic Virus
- ❑ Potato Virus Y

- ❑ Tomato Spotted Wilt Virus
- ❑ Cucumber Mosaic Virus
- ❑ Tobacco Etch Virus
- ❑ Tobacco Vein Mottling Virus
- ❑ Alfalfa Mosaic Virus
- ❑ Tobacco Curl Leaf Virus

Diseases Caused by Parasitic Plants

- ❑ Broomrape
- ❑ Witchweed
- ❑ Dodder

An exceptional book on this subject, *Compendium of Tobacco Diseases,* is available for sale from APS Press, either online or writing to them:

3340 Pilot Knob Road,
St. Paul, MN 55121
United States

Toll-Free: 800-328-7560 United States and most of Canada
Phone: 651-454-7250
Fax: 651-454-0766

Images of all tobacco diseases can also be found at www.forestryimages.org.

Chapter 7

SAVING SEEDS

Heirloom nicotiana is a prolific seed producer. To collect seeds, simply open the dried flower seedpods and hundreds will spill out. It takes about a teaspoon of seeds to plant an acre of tobacco. One-half ounce of seeds is about 150,000 seeds or enough to cover two to five acres.

Nursery hybrid types must have new seeds every season. If you collect these seeds, the second generation the following summer will be very disappointing.

Because 90 percent of heirloom nicotiana flowers are self-fertilizing, the chances of cross-pollination are minimal. However, if you are planning to collect seeds and are planting several varieties in close proximity to one another, to prevent accidental cross-pollination, the flowers should be bagged prior to opening. Bagging will ensure that future generations are true to the original. You will only need to bag one or maybe two plants to collect more than enough seeds.

Seed-collecting bags can be made of several different materials. Mesh gift bags, found at craft supply chain stores, under the name of Organza Bags, are ideal. Old nylon stocking will work too. Mesh bags can be made from bridal veil material also found in craft stores.

The bags should be placed over the flowers before they open, as illustrated in the photograph below. Remove a few layers of the leaves below the flowers so they won't interfere with tying the bag to the stem.

Photo: Beth Pocker ©

Bags would be used to cover the flowers at this stage.

Cut away some of the leaves under the emerging flower head to be able to tie the bag to the stem.

Mesh Seed Bags

Pantyhose Seed Bags

In the photo below, there are about twenty-five different varieties of heirloom nicotiana in close proximity to each other. If I had intended to save seeds, each one of them would require a seed bag to prevent cross-pollination. In this case, I just wanted to enjoy the beauty of the plants, and I discarded them at the end of the season without collecting the seeds.

Photo: Richard Pocker ©

To save the seeds of these twenty-five different varieties without risking cross-pollination, every plant would need to be bagged.

Appendix A

SEED SOURCES AND CONTACT INFORMATION

Adaptive Seeds
adaptiveseeds.com
25079 Brush Creek
Sweet Home, OR 97386
Tel. 541-367-1105

Annie's Annuals
anniesannuals.com
801 Chesley Ave
Richmond, CA 94801
Tel. 888-226-4370

Allies
alliesonline.net
PO Box 2422
Sebastopol, CA 95473

Botanical Spirit
Canada
botanicalspirit.com
PO Box 88504
Surrey, BC
V3W 0X1 Canada
Tel. 778-239-7892

Botanical Interests
botanicalinterests.com
660 Compton Street
Broomfield, CO 80020
Tel. 877-821-4340

Baker Creek Heirloom Seeds
rareseeds.com
2278 Baker Creek
Mansfield, MO 65704
Tel. 417-924-8917

B&T World Seeds
France
b-and-t-world-seeds.com
Paguigan
34210 Aigues-Vives
France
Tel. 0033(0)4 68912039

D.T. Brown, UK
dtbrownseeds.co.uk
Bury Road
Newmarket CB87PQ
England
Tel. 0845 371 1032

W. Atlee Burpee
burpee.com
300 Park Ave
Warminster, PA 18974
Tel. 800-888-1447

Chileflora
chileflora.com
2 Sur 655
Dpto 208
Talca Chile

Cibergarden-Spain
cibergarden.com
Web only

Chiltern Seeds, UK
chilternseeds.co.uk
Crowmarsh Battle Barns
114 Preston Crowmarsh
Wallingford
OX10 6SL, UK
Tel. 44(0) 1491 824675

Cross Creek Coating
crosscreekseeds.com
2000 Vass Rd
Raeford, NC 28376
Tel. 910-904-5588
COMMERCIAL SEEDS ONLY

Crocus, UK
crocus.co.uk
Nursery Court
London Road
Windlesham
Surrey GU20 6LQ
England
Tel. 01344 578 000

Connecticut Valley Tobacco Historical Society
tobaccohistsoc.org
135 Lang Rd
Windsor, CT 06095
Tel. 860-285-1888

Daggawalla
daggawalla.com
9035 SE Washington St
Portland, OR 97216
Tel. 503-686-5557

De Werkplaats Netherlands
de-werkplaats.info
1st Mientlaan 13
2223 LG Katwijk
Netherlands
No phone. PLANTS ONLY

Dobies of Devon
dobies.co.uk
Long Road
Paignton
Devon TQ4 7SX
England
Tel. 0844-701-7625

Dave's Garden
davesgarden.com
Web only
Excellent source of information and trading of seeds

eBay
ebay.com
Web only
Excellent source of seeds for sale

Diane's Seeds
dianeseeds.com
1380 N. Hwy 89
Ogden, UT 84404
No phone

Fair Trade Tobacco Seed Bank
fairtradetobacco.com
Web-only source for seed trading and purchase

Mr. Fothergill's, UK
mr-fothergills.co.uk
Gazeley Road
Kentford
Suffolk CB8 7QB
England
Tel. 0845-371-0518

Greta's Canada
seeds-organic.com
399 River Road
Gloucester ON
K1V 1C9 Canada
Tel. 613-521-8648

Glacier Gardens
glaciergardenursery.com
9148 James Blvd
Juneau, AK 99801
Tel.907-789-5166
PLANTS ONLY

Henry Field's Seeds
henryfields.com
PO Box 397
Aurora, IN 47001
Tel. 513-354-1495

Harris Seeds
harrisseeds.com
PO Box 24966
Rochester, NY 14624
Tel. 800-544-7938

Hart's Greenhouse
hartsgreenhouseflorist.com
43 Clinton Ave
Norwich, CT 06360
Tel. 860-546-6541
Other locations in CT—Canterbury and Brooklyn

Heirloom Tobacco
heirloomtobacco.com
Web only

J.L. Hudson
hudsonseeds.com
PO Box 337
La Honda, CA 94020
No phone. One of the most informative seed catalogs.

Heavenly Products
heavenly-products.com
Web only

Hazzard's
hazzardsgreenhouse.com
PO Box 151
Deford, MI 48729
Tel.989-872-5057
Wholesale but no minimum order required.

Horizon Herbs
horizonherbs.com
PO Box 69
Williams, OR 97544
Tel. 541-846-6704

Horticulture Products & Services
hpsseed.com
334 W. Stroud St
Ste. 1
Randolph WI 53956
Tel. 800-322-7288

Hardy Plants
hardyplants.com
481 Reflection Rd
Apple Valley, MN 55124
Tel. 952-432-8673

Impecta Sweden
impecta.se
SE-643
98 Julita Sweden
Tel. 046 (0) 150-92331

King Seeds
kingseeds.co.nz
PO Box 283
Katikati 3166
Bay of Plenty NZ
Tel. 07 549 3409

Magic Garden Seeds Germany
magicgardenseeds.com
Andreas Fai-Pozar
93053 Regensburg
Germany
No phone

Moles Seeds, UK
molessseeds.com
Turkey Cock Lane
Stanway
Colchester
Essex CO3 8PD
England
Tel. 044 (0) 1206-213213

Nicky's Nursery, UK
nickys-nursery.co.uk
Fairfield Rd
Broadstairs
Kent CT10 2JU
England
Tel. 01843 600972

Nuts n Cones
nutsncones.co.uk
35 Leverstock Green Rd.
Hemel Hempstead

Hertfordshire
HP2 4HH
England
Tel. 01442 260 237

Northwood Seeds
northwoodseeds.com
4724 E. Mount Spokane Park Dr.
Mead, WA 99021
Tel. 502-466-0942

Native Seeds
nativeseeds.org
3061 N. Campbell Ave
Tucson, AZ 85719
Tel. 520-622-5561

New Hope Seeds
newhopeseed.com
PO Box 443
Bon Aqua, TN 37025
No phone

Notcutts, UK
notcutts.co.uk
Cumberland 8
Woodbridge
Suffolk
1P12 4AF
Tel. 0844879 4166

Organica Seed
organicaseedco.com
PO Box 611
Wilbraham, MA

01095
Tel. 413-283-6463

Plant World Seeds
plant-world-seeds.com
St. Marychurch Rd., Newton Abbot, Devon TQ12 4SE, UK
44 (0) 1803 872939

Rostliny-Semena
Czech Republic
rostliny-semena.cz/cz
Luke Tobolak
Masaryk 60
Luhacouice 76326
Czech Republic
No phone

Richbar Canada
richbarnursery.com
3028 Red Bluff
Quesnel BC
V2J 6C6
Canada
Tel. 250-747-2915

Sacred Succulents
sacredsucculents.com
PO Box 781
Sebastopol, CA
95473
No phone

Sarah Raven, UK
sarahraven.com
Web or phone only
Tel. 0845 092 0283

Suttons Seeds, UK
seeds.Suttons.co.uk
Web or phone only
Tel. 0333 400 2899

Seedaholic Ireland
seedaholic.com
Ballintleva
Clogher
Westport Co.
Mayo Ireland
No phone

Swallowtail Gardens
swallowtailgardenseeds.com
122 Calistoga Rd #178
Costa Rosa, CA
95409
1877 489 7333

Special Plants, UK
specialplants.net
Greenways Lane
Cold Ashton
Wilts SN14 8LA
England Tel. 01225 891 686

Seedman, UK
seedman.com
Web only
Ships, UK only

Summer Hill Seeds
summerhillseeds.com
13505 Hamilton Pike Rd
Whittington, IL
62897
Tel. 206-203-3455

Sustainable Seeds
sustainableseed.com
PO Box 38
Covelo, CA
95428
Tel. 877 620 7333

Seeds of Eaden, UK
seedsofeaden.co.uk
Web only
Website has interesting history of seed hunters.

Seed Tapestry
seedtapestry.com
Web only

Silene Belgium
silene.be
Dear Andriaensens
Bosstraat128
9255 Buggenhout
Belgium
Tel. 32(52) 336 404

Select Seeds
selectseeds.com
180 Stickney Hill Rd
Union, CT 06076
Tel. 800-684-0395

Thompson & Morgan
thompson-morgan.com
Web and retailers
Website will direct you to the correct site for your location

The Tobacco Seed Co., UK
thetobaccoseed.com
110 South Ave
Southend on Sea
Essex SS2 4HU
England
No phone

Terrapin Gardens
terrapin-gardens.com
Web only

Terroir Seeds
underwoodgardens.com
PO Box 4995
Chino Valley, AZ 86323
Tel. 888-878-5247

Von Trapp Greenhouse
vontrappgreenhouse.com
208 Common Rd
Waitsfield, VT
05673

Tel. 802-496-4385
PLANTS ONLY

Virginia Tobacco Seeds
virginiatobaccoseeds.com
Web only

Victory Seeds
victoryseeds.com
PO Box 192
Molalla, OR
97038
Tel. 503-829-3126
Voice mail

White Flower Farm
whiteflowerfarm.com
PO Box 50
Route 53
Litchfield, CT 06759
Tel. 800-503-9624

Workman Tobacco Seed
workmantobacco.com
7046 St. Rt. 94 W
W. Murray, KY 42071
Tel. 270-435-4096
Commercial Supplier

West Seed Farm
westseedfarm.com
3225 Drew St
Los Angeles, CA 90065
No phone

Wasco Nursery
wasconursery.com
41 W 781 Rt. 64
St. Charles, IL 60175
Tel. 630-584-4424
PLANTS ONLY

COMPLETE LIST OF NICOTIANA SEEDS AND SOURCES

Acuminata-Chileflora.com
Acuminata-Daggawalla
Adonis-Virginia Tobacco Seeds, Spain
Adonis -Sustainable Seeds
Affinis-Chiltern, UK
Affinis-Cibergarden, Spain
Affinis-Crocus
Affinis-Dobies, UK
Affinis-Northwood Seeds
Affinis-Nuts n Cones, UK
Affinis-Plant World Seeds, UK
Affinis-Richbar (plants only)
Affinis-Sutton Seeds, UK
Affinis-Victory Seeds
Affinis-Virginia Tobacco Seeds, Spain
Affinis-White Flower Farms (plants only)
African Red-Northwood Seeds
African Red-Sustainable Seeds
African Red-The Tobacco Seed Company
African Red-Virginia Tobacco Seeds, Spain
Ahus-Northwood Seeds
Ahus-Sustainable Seeds

Alida-Swedish -Virginia Tobacco Seeds, Spain
American 14-Northwood Seeds
American 14-Sustainable Seeds
American 572-Northwood Seeds
Avalon Appleblossom-B&T
Avalon Appleblossom-Hazzard's Seed Store
Avalon Appleblossom-Impecta, Sweden
Avalon Appleblossom-Moles Seeds, UK
Avalon Appleblossom-Nuts n Cones, UK
Avalon Appleblossom-Pase Seeds
Avalon Appleblosson-Seed Tapestry
Avalon Bright Pink-Dobies, UK
Avalon Bright Pink-Seed Tapestry
Avalon Burgundy-Hazzard's Seed Store
Avalon Burgundy-Pase Seeds
Avalon Burgundy-Seed Tapestry
Avalon Lime-B&T
Avalon Lime-Hazzard's Seed Store
Avalon Lime-Moles Seeds, UK
Avalon Lime-Nuts n Cones, UK
Avalon Lime-Pase Seeds
Avalon Lime-Seed Tapestry
Avalon Lime & Purple Bicolor-B&T
Avalon Lime & Purple Bicolor-Seed Tapestry
Avalon Lime-Purple Bicolor-Nuts n Cones, UK
Avalon Lime-Purple Bicolor-Hazzard's Seed Store
Avalon Lime-Purple Bicolor-Summer Hill
Avalon Mixed-D T Brown, UK
Avalon Mixed-Harris Seeds
Avalon Mixed-Hazzard's Seed Store
Avalon Mixed-Nut n Cones, UK
Avalon Mixed-Swallowtail
Avalon Mixed Dwarf-B&T
Avalon Peach-Seed Tapestry
Avalon Picotee-Impecta, Sweden

Avalon Pink Picotee-B&T
Avalon Pink Picotee-Nuts n Cones, UK
Avalon Pink Picotee-Seed Tapestry
Avalon Pink Picotee-Summer Hill
Avalon Red-B&T
Avalon Red-Hazzard's Seed Store
Avalon Red-Nuts n Cones, UK
Avalon Red-Pase Seeds
Avalon Red-Seed Tapestry
Avalon White-B&T
Avalon White-Hazzard's Seed Store
Avalon White-Impecta, Sweden
Avalon White-Nuts n Cones, UK
Avalon White-Pase Seeds
Avalon White-Seed Tapestry
Aztec-Northwood Seeds
Babybella-Hazzard's Seed Store
Babybella-Henry Field's Seeds
Babybella-Nicky's, UK
Babybella-Park Seeds
Babybella-Silene, Belgium
Babybella-Summer Hill
Babybella-Von Trapp Greenhouse (plants only)
Babybella Antique Red-Swallowtail
Bafra-Daggawalla
Bafra-New Hope
Bafra-Northwood Seeds
Bafra-Sustainable Seeds
Baiano-Northwood Seeds
Baiano-Virginia Tobacco Seeds, Spain
Baiano-Sustainable Seeds
Baino-Daggawalla
Balikesir-Northwood Seeds
Balikesir-Virginia Tobacco Seeds, Spain
Balikesir-Sustainable Seeds

Bamboo Shoot-Northwood Seeds
Bamboo Shoot-Virginia Tobacco Seeds, Spain
Bamboo Shoot-Sustainable Seeds
Banana Leaf-New Hope
Banana Leaf-Northwood Seeds
Banana Leaf-The Tobacco Seed Co., UK
Banana Leaf-Virginia Tobacco Seeds, Spain
Banana Leaf-West Seed Farm
Banana Leaf-Sustainable Seeds
Barinas-Heirloom Tobacco
Barinas-Tobacco Seed Co., UK
Barnett Special-New Hope
Basma-Cibergarden Spain
Basma-The Tobacco Seed Co., UK
Basma-Virginia Tobacco Seeds, Spain
Bedder Crimson-B&T
Big Gem-New Hope
Big Gem-Northwood Seeds
Big Gem-The Tobacco Seed Co., UK
Big Gem-West Seed Farm
Big Gem-Sustainable Seeds
Big Love Bigelovii-Allies
Big Love Bigelovii-Daggawalla
Black Knight-De Werkplaats, Netherlands
Black Knight-Sarah Raven, UK
Black Knight-Silene, Belgium
Black Sea Samsun-Daggawalla
Black Sea Samsun-Greta's
Black Sea Samsun-Northwood Seeds
Black Sea Samsun-The Tobacco Seed Co., UK
Black Sea Samsun-Sustainable Seeds
Bolivian Black-Virginia Tobacco Seeds, Spain
Bolivian Criollo Black-Northwood Seeds
Bolivian Criollo Black-Sustainable Seeds
Bonanza-New Hope

Bonanza-West Seed Farm
Bosikappal-Heirloom Tobacco
Bosikappal-Northwood Seeds
Bosikappal-Sustainable Seeds
Brown Leaf-B&T
Brown Leaf-JL Hudson
Brown Leaf-Rostliny-Semena, Czech
Brown Leaf-Semena-Osvia, Slovakia
Bucak-Northwood Seeds
Bucak-Sustainable Seeds
Burley-Chiltern, UK
Burley-Greta's
Burley-Magic Garden Seeds
Burley-The Tobacco Seed Co., UK
Burley 21-Northwood Seeds
Burley 21-Sustainable Seeds
Burley 64-Northwood Seeds
Burley 64-Sustainable Seeds
Burley Deutschland-Virginia Tobacco Seeds, Spain
Burley Gold Dollar-New Hope
Burley Gold Dollar-Northwood Seeds
Burley Gold Dollar-The Tobacco Seed Co., UK
Burley Gold Seal-Greta's
Burley Golden Burley-New Hope
Burley Golden Burley-Northwood Seeds
Burley Golden Burley-The Tobacco Seed Co., UK
Burley Golden Burley-Victory Seeds
Burley Green Brior-New Hope
Burley Green Brior-Northwood Seeds
Burley Green Brior-West Seed Farm
Burley Harrow Velvet-New Hope
Burley Harrow Velvet-Northwood Seeds
Burley Harrow Velvet-Sustainable Seeds
Burley Harrow Velvet-The Tobacco Seed Co., UK
Burley Harrow Velvet-Virginia Tobacco Seeds, Spain

Burley Kentucky-Semena-Osvia, Slovakia
Burley KY 14-JL Hudson
Burley KY 17-B&T
Burley KY 17-JL Hudson
Burley KY 21-New Hope
Burley KY 21-West Seed Farm
Burley KY 5-New Hope
Burley KY 5-West Seed Farm
Burley KY 907-JL Hudson
Burley Monte Calme Blonde-The Tobacco Seed Co., UK
Burley Monte Calme Yellow-B&T
Burley Monte Calme Yellow-Northwood Seeds
Burley Tennessee-Organica
Burley TN 86-JL Hudson
Burley TN 86-Northwood Seeds
Burley TN 86-Victory Seeds
Burley TN 86LC-Northwood Seeds
Burley TN 90-Semena-Osvia, Slovakia
Burley TN 90-B&T
Burley TN 90-Cibergarden, Spain
Burley TN 90-JL Hudson
Burley TN 90 -Northwood Seeds
Burley TN 90-Virginia Tobacco Seeds, Spain
Burley TN 90LC-Northwood Seeds
Burley TND 950-JL Hudson
Burley Virginia 509-JL Hudson
Burley Virginia 509-Northwood Seeds
Burley Yellow Twist Bud-New Hope
Burley Yellow Twist Bud-Northwood Seeds
Burley Yellow Twist Bud-Victory Seeds
Burley Yellow Twist Bud-West Seed Farm
Bursa-Northwood Seeds
Bursa-Sustainable Seeds
Catterton-Northwood Seeds
Catterton-The Tobacco Seed Co., UK

Catterton-Victory Seeds
Catterton-Virginia Tobacco Seeds, Spain
Catterton-West Seed Farm
Catterton-Sustainable Seeds
Celikhan-Northwood Seeds
Celikhan-Sustainable Seeds
Cherry Red-Northwood Seeds
Cherry Red -Sustainable Seeds
Chilean -Sustainable Seeds
Cimarron-Solaniflora-Chileflora.com, Chile
Cimarron-Solaniflora-Daggawalla
Clevelandii-New Hope
Clevelandii-Northwood Seeds
Clevelandii-Victory Seeds
Coker 371-Northwood Seeds
Comstock Spanish-New Hope
Comstock Spanish-Northwood Seeds
Comstock Spanish-West Seed Farm
Connecticut 49-Northwood Seeds
Connecticut Broadleaf-New Hope
Connecticut Broadleaf-Northwood Seeds
Connecticut Broadleaf-Sustainable Seeds
Connecticut Broadleaf-The Tobacco Seed Co., UK
Connecticut Broadleaf-Victory Seeds
Connecticut Broadleaf-West Seed Farm
Connecticut Shade-B&T
Connecticut Shade-New Hope
Connecticut Shade-Northwood Seeds
Connecticut Wrapper-Adaptive Seeds
Costa Rica-Virginia Tobacco Seeds, Spain
Costa Rica 589-Northwood Seeds
Costello-Northwood Seeds
Costello-Sustainable Seeds
Coyote attenuata-Allies
Coyote attenuata-Daggawalla

Crimea-Sustainable Seeds
Crimean-Northwood Seeds
Crimson Bedder-Chiltern, UK
Crimson Bedder-Select Seeds
Crimson Bedder-The Flower Company (plants only)
Crimson Red-Seedaholic
Criollo-Heirloom Tobacco
Criollo-Sustainable Seeds
Criollo-The Tobacco Seed Co., UK
Criollo 98-Northwood Seeds
Criollo 98-Virginia Tobacco Seeds, Spain
Cuba 4-Northwood Seeds
Cuba 4-Sustainable Seeds
Dark Virginia-Virginia Tobacco Seeds, Spain
Daule-Heirloom Tobacco
Daule-Northwood Seeds
Daule-Sustainable Seeds
Daylight Sensation-Richbar (plants only)
Del Gold-B&T
Del Gold-Nicky's, UK only
Del Gold-Northwood Seeds
Del Gold-The Tobacco Seed Co., UK
Delgold-Sustainable Seeds
Desert Suaveolens-Silene, Belgium
Desert Trigonophylla-Heavenly Products
Desert Trigonophylla-Horizon Herbs
Dixie Bright 27-Northwood Seeds
Dixie Shade-New Hope
Dixie Shade-West Seed Farm
Dogon-Daggawalla
Dominican Republic-Northwood Seeds
Dominican Republic-Sustainable Seeds
Domino-Portland Nursery (plants only)
Domino Antique Shades-Nicky's (UK only)
Domino Mixed-Dobies, UK

Domino Mixed-Hazzard's Seed Store
Domino Mixed-HPS
Domino Mixed-Richbar (plants only)
Domino Salmon Pink-Hazzard's Seed Store
Domino Salmon Pink-Summer Hill
Domino Salmon Pink-Von Trapp Greenhouse (plants only)
Domino White-Hazzard's Seed Store
Dukat Crimean-Northwood Seeds
Dukat Crimean-Sustainable Seeds
Dwarf White Bedder-Thompson & Morgan, UK
Eau de Cologne Mixed-Thompson & Morgan, US & UK
Florida 17-Northwood Seeds
Florida 17-Sustainable Seeds
Florida Sumatra-New Hope
Florida Sumatra-Northwood Seeds
Florida Sumatra-West Seed Farm
Flowering Mutabilis-Diane Seeds
Flowering Mutabilis-JL Hudson
Flowering Mutabilis-Sarah Raven, UK
Fragrant Cloud-Daggawalla
Fragrant Cloud-De Werkplaats Netherlands
Fragrant Cloud-Diane's Seeds
Fragrant Cloud-Hazzard's Seed Store
Fragrant Cloud-Plant World Seeds, UK
Fragrant Cloud-Seedman.com (UK only)
Fragrant Cloud-Silene, Belgium
Fragrant Cloud-Thompson & Morgan, US & UK
Fragrant Delight-Hardy Plants
Frog Eye Orinoco-New Hope
Glessnor-West Seed Farm
Glessnor or Glessner-New Hope
Glutinosa-B&T
Glutinosa-Impecta, Sweden
Glutinosa-JL Hudson
Glutinosa-Nicky's, UK

Glutinosa-Silene, Belgium
Glutinosa-The Flower Company (plants only)
Glutinosa-Virginia Tobacco Seeds, Spain
Gold Dollar-Sustainable Seeds
Gold Leaf 939-Northwood Seeds
Gold Leaf Orinoco-Heirloom Tobacco
Gold Leaf Orinoco-Northwood Seeds
Gold Leaf Orinoco-Sustainable Seeds
Golden Burley-Sustainable Seeds
Golden Wilt-Northwood Seeds
Golden Wilt-Sustainable Seeds
Goose Creek Red-Northwood Seeds
Goose Creek Red-Sustainable Seeds
Grand Ol' White Alata-Seedman.com (UK only)
Grandiflora-Impecta, Sweden
Grandiflora-Sarah Raven, UK
Grandiflora-Swallowtail
Green Brior-Sustainable Seeds
Greenwood-B&T
Greenwood-JL Hudson
Greenwood-New Hope
Greenwood-Northwood Seeds
Greenwood-Organica
Greenwood-The Tobacco Seed Co., UK
Greenwood-Victory Seeds
Habano-Heirloom Tobacco
Habano 2000-Northwood Seeds
Habano 2000-Sustainable Seeds
Hacienda de cura habano-Canary Island-Cibergarden Spain
Hacienda del Cura-Virginia Tobacco Seeds, Spain
Havana-Cibergarden Spain
Havana 142-B&T
Havana 142-JL Hudson
Havana 142-Northwood Seeds
Havana 142-Sustainable Seeds

Havana 142-The Tobacco Seed Co., UK
Havana 263-New Hope
Havana 503-Organica
Havana 608-B&T
Havana 608-Greta's
Havana 608-JL Hudson
Havana 608-Northwood Seeds
Havana 608-Organica
Havana 608-Sustainable Seeds
Havana-Carmine Red Hybrid-Richbar (plants only)
Havana-Cuba Mixed Hybrid-Nicky's, UK
Havana-Lilac Rose Hybrid-Hardy Plants
Havana Z 299-Sustainable Seeds
Havana Z299-Northwood Seeds
Heaven Scent-Burpee
Helena-Northwood Seeds
Helena-Sustainable Seeds
Hickory Prior-New Hope
Hickory Prior-Northwood Seeds
Hickory Prior-West Seed Farm
Hickory Prior-Sustainable Seeds
Homestead-Sustainable Seeds
Hot Chocolate-Nicky's, UK
Hot Chocolate-Special Plants, UK
Hot Chocolate-Terrapin Gardens (plants only)
Hot Chocolate-The Flower Company (plants only)
Hummingbird Lilac-Richbar (plants only)
Improved Madole-JL Hudson
Improved Madole-West Seed Farm
Indian -Sustainable Seeds
Indian-Quadrivalvis-Northwood Seeds
Indian-Quadrivalvis-Sustainable Seeds
Isleta Pueblo-Sustainable Seeds
Italian-Sustainable Seeds
Izmir-Cibergarden, Spain

Izmir-Virginia Tobacco Seeds, Spain
Izmir Lebanese-Northwood Seeds
Izmir Ozbis-Northwood Seeds
Izmir Ozbis-Sustainable Seeds
Izmir-Turkish-The Tobacco Seed Co., UK
Japan 8-Northwood Seeds
Japan 8-Sustainable Seeds
Jasmine-Crocus
Jasmine-Diane's
Jasmine-Sustainable Seeds
Jasmine-alata var. Grandiflora-Allies
Jasmine-alata var. Grandiflora-B&T
Jasmine-alata var. Grandiflora-Diane's Seeds
Jasmine-alata var. Grandiflora-JL Hudson
Jasmine-alata var. Grandiflora-Northwood Seeds
Jasmine-alata var. Grandiflora-Seedaholic
Jasmine-alata var. Grandiflora-Seedman.com (UK only)
Jasmine-alata var. Grandiflora-Select Seeds
Jasmine-alata var. Grandiflora-Special Plants, UK
Jasmine-alata var. Grandiflora-Terroir Seeds
Jasmine-alata var. Grandiflora-The Flower Company (plants only)
Jasmine-alata var. Grandiflora-Victory Seeds
Kelly Brownleaf-New Hope
Kelly Brownleaf-West Seed Farm
Kelly Burley-New Hope
Kelly Burley-Victory Seeds
Kentucky-Magic Garden Seeds
Kentucky-Semena-Osvia, Slovakia
Kessu-Sustainable Seeds
Knightiana-B&T
Knightiana-Hazzard's Seed Store
Knightiana-Plant World Seeds, UK
Knightiana-Portland Nursery (plants only)
Knightiana-Seedman.com (UK only)
Knightiana-Silene, Belgium

Knightiana-Special Plants, UK
Knightiana-The Flower Company (plants only)
Kumanovo-Northwood Seeds
Kumanovo-Virginia Tobacco Seeds, Spain
Kumanovo-Sustainable Seeds
KY 15-Northwood Seeds
KY 15-Sustainable Seeds
KY 17-Northwood Seeds
KY 17-Sustainable Seeds
KY 171-JL Hudson
KY 190-Northwood Seeds
KY 190-Sustainable Seeds
KY 8635-Northwood Seeds
KY 8635-Sustainable Seeds
Lancaster Seed Leaf-Northwood Seeds
Lancaster Seedleaf-New Hope
Lancaster Seedleaf-Sustainable Seeds
Lancaster Seedleaf-West Seed Farm
Langsdorfii-B&T
Langsdorfii-Baker Creek
Langsdorfii-Botanical Interests
Langsdorfii-Chiltern, UK
Langsdorfii-De Werkplaats, Netherlands
Langsdorfii-Hardy Plants
Langsdorfii-Hazzard's Seed Store
Langsdorfii-Hazzard's Seed Store
Langsdorfii-Heavenly Products
Langsdorfii-Horizon Herbs
Langsdorfii-Impecta, Sweden
Langsdorfii-Northwood Seeds
Langsdorfii-Plant World Seeds, UK
Langsdorfii-Portland Nursery (plants only)
Langsdorfii-Seedman.com (UK only)
Langsdorfii-Select Seeds
Langsdorfii-Silene, Belgium

Langsdorfii-Special Plants, UK
Langsdorfii-Swallowtail
Langsdorfii-Terroir Seeds
Langsdorfii-Terroir Seeds
Langsdorfii-The Flower Company (plants only)
Langsdorfii-Thompson & Morgan, US & UK
Langsdorfii-Von Trapp Greenhouse (plants only)
Langsdorfii-White Flower Farms (plants only)
Langsdorfii-Cream Splash-B&T
Langsdorfii-Cream Splash-Nicky's, UK
Langsdorfii-Cream Splash-Plant World Seeds, UK
Langsdorfii-Cream Splash-Chiltern, UK
Lime Green-B&T
Lime Green-Baker Creek
Lime Green-Chiltern, UK
Lime Green-Crocus
Lime Green-De Werkplaats, Netherlands
Lime Green-DT Brown, UK
Lime Green-Hardy Plants
Lime Green-Hazzard's Seed Store
Lime Green-Impecta, Sweden
Lime Green-Nicky's, UK
Lime Green-Nuts n Cones, UK
Lime Green-Sarah Raven, UK
Lime Green-Seedaholic
Lime Green-Seedman.com (UK only)
Lime Green-Silene, Belgium
Lime Green-Special Plants, UK
Lime Green-The Flower Company (plants only)
Little Crittenden-JL Hudson
Little Crittenden-Organica
Little Crittenden-Sustainable Seeds
Little Crittenden-Terroir Seeds
Little Crittenden-The Tobacco Seed Co., UK
Little Cuba-Northwood Seeds

Little Cuba-Sustainable Seeds
Little Dutch-Heirloom Tobacco
Little Dutch-New Hope
Little Dutch-Northwood Seeds
Little Dutch-Sustainable Seeds
Little Dutch-Victory Seeds
Little Dutch-Virginia Tobacco Seeds, Spain
Little Wood-B&T
Little Wood-JL Hudson
Little Wood-Semena-Osvia, Slovakia
Little Yellow Seed-New Hope
Lizard Tail Orinoco-B&T
Lizard Tail Orinoco-JL Hudson
Lizard Tail Orinoco-New Hope
Lizard Tail Orinoco-The Tobacco Seed Co., UK
Lizard Tail Orinoco-West Seed Farm
Lizard Tail Orinoco x Turtle Foot-B&T
Lizard Tail Orinoco x Turtle Foot-JL Hudson
Lizard Tail Orinoco x Turtle Foot-The Tobacco Seed Co., UK
Lizard Tail Orinoco x Turtle Foot-West Seed Farm
Long Red-New Hope
Long Red-Northwood Seeds
Long Red-Sustainable Seeds
Madole-Heirloom Tobacco
Madole-New Hope
Madole-Northwood Seeds
Madole-Semena-Osvia, Slovakia
Madole-Sustainable Seeds
Madole Improved-B&T
Madole Narrow Leaf-JL Hudson
Madole-Narrow Leaf-Organica
Madole Tom Ross-B&T
Madole Tom Ross-JL Hudson
Magnolia-Northwood Seeds
Magnolia-Sustainable Seeds

Mammoth Black-JL Hudson
Mammoth Black-The Tobacco Seed Co., UK
Mammoth White-Northwood Seeds
Mammoth White-West Seed Farm
Mammoth Yellow-New Hope
Mammoth Yellow-West Seed Farm
Maritima-Chiltern, UK
Maritima-Daggawalla
Maritima-Silene, Belgium
Marshmallow-*See Mutabilis*
Maryland-The Tobacco Seed Co., UK
Maryland-Keller -New Hope
Maryland-Keller-West Seed Farm
MD 609-Northwood Seeds
MD 609-Virginia Tobacco Seeds, Spain
MD 609-Sustainable Seeds
MD A30-Northwood Seeds
MD A30-Sustainable Seeds
Merlin Salmon Pink-Richbar (plants only)
Monte Calme Brun-Greta's
Monte Calme Brun-Organica
Monte Calme Yellow-Northwood Seeds
Monte Calme Yellow-Sustainable Seeds
Monte Calme Yellow-The Tobacco Seed Co, UK
Monte Calme Yellow-Virginia Tobacco Seeds, Spain
Moonlight-Northwood Seeds
Moonlight-Sustainable Seeds
Mostrenco-Northwood Seeds
Mostrenco-Sustainable Seeds
Mutabilis-B&T
Mutabilis-B&T
Mutabilis-Burpee
Mutabilis-Chiltern, UK
Mutabilis-Daggawalla
Mutabilis-De Werkplaats, Netherlands

Mutabilis-Hazzard's Seed Store
Mutabilis-Impecta, Sweden
Mutabilis-Portland Nursery (plants only)
Mutabilis-Seedman.com (UK only)
Mutabilis-Silene, Belgium
Mutabilis-Special Plants, UK
Mutabilis-Thompson & Morgan, US & UK
Ohio Dutch-Sustainable Seeds
Okanawa-Northwood Seeds
Okinawa-Sustainable Seeds
One Sucker-JL Hudson
One Sucker-New Hope
One Sucker-Northwood Seeds
One Sucker-Sustainable Seeds
One Sucker-Victory Seeds
One Sucker-West Seed Farm
Ontario Bold CT 572-B&T
Ontario Light CT 157-B&T
Orinoco-Northwood Seeds
Orinoco-Organica
Orinoco-Sustainable Seeds
Orinoco-The Tobacco Seed Co., UK
Orinoco-Virginia Tobacco Seeds, Spain
Orinoco Lizard Tail-Semena-Osvia, Slovakia
OS 400-JL Hudson
Oxford 027-Northwood Seeds
Oxford 207-Sustainable Seeds
Paniculata-Hazzard's Seed Store
Paniculata-Seedman.com (UK only)
Papante-Northwood Seeds
Papante -Sustainable Seeds
Paris Wrapper-New Hope
Paris Wrapper-Northwood Seeds
Paris Wrapper-West Seed Farm
Paris Wrapper-Sustainable Seeds

Pennbel-Northwood Seeds
Pennbel 69-Sustainable Seeds
Pennsylvania Red-New Hope
Pennsylvania Red-Northwood Seeds
Pennsylvania Red-Seedman.com (UK only)
Pennsylvania Red-Sustainable Seeds
Pennsylvania Red-Virginia Tobacco Seeds, Spain
Perfume Antique Lime-Nuts n Cones, UK
Perfume Antique Lime-Seed Tapestry
Perfume Antique Lime-Silene, Belgium
Perfume Antique Lime-Swallowtail
Perfume Blue-Glacier Gardens (plants only)
Perfume Blue-Hazzard's Seed Store
Perfume Blue-Nuts n Cones, UK
Perfume Blue-Seed Tapestry
Perfume Blue-Silene, Belgium
Perfume Blue-Summer Hill
Perfume Bright Rose-Hazzard's Seed Store
Perfume Bright Rose-Nuts n Cones, UK
Perfume Bright Rose-Seed Tapestry
Perfume Deep Purple-Hardy Plants
Perfume Deep Purple-Hazzard's Seed Store
Perfume Deep Purple-HPS
Perfume Deep Purple-Nuts n Cones, UK
Perfume Deep Purple-Park Seeds
Perfume Deep Purple-Seed Tapestry
Perfume Deep Purple-Select Seeds
Perfume Deep Purple-Swallowtail
Perfume Deep Purple-Thompson & Morgan, US & UK
Perfume Lilac-Seed Tapestry
Perfume Lime-Hazzard's Seed Store
Perfume Lime-Summer Hill
Perfume Lime Green-Von Trapp Greenhouse (plants only)
Perfume Mixed-D T Brown, UK
Perfume Mixed-Hardy Plants

Perfume Mixed-Harris Seeds
Perfume Mixed-Hazzard's Seed Store
Perfume Mixed-J.W. Jung
Perfume Mixed-Nicky's, UK
Perfume Mixed-Nuts n Cones, UK
Perfume Mixed-Park Seeds
Perfume Mixed-Seed Tapestry
Perfume Mixed-Suttons Seeds, UK
Perfume Mixed-Swallowtail
Perfume Mixed-Von Trapp Greenhouse (plants only)
Perfume Purple-Sarah Raven, UK
Perfume Purple-Silene, Belgium
Perfume Purple-Special Plants, UK
Perfume Red-Hazzard's Seed Store
Perfume Red-Nuts n Cones, UK
Perfume Red-Seed Tapestry
Perfume Red-Silene, Belgium
Perfume Red-Summer Hill
Perfume White -Hazzard's Seed Store
Perfume White-Nuts n Cones, UK
Perfume White-Seed Tapestry
Perfume White-Silene, Belgium
Perfume White-Swallowtail
Pergeu Brazil-Northwood Seeds
Pergeu-Brazil-Sustainable Seeds
Perique-B&T
Perique-Baker Creek
Perique-Greta's
Perique-JL Hudson
Perique-New Hope
Perique-The Tobacco Seed Co., UK
Perique-Victory Seeds
Polish-Northwood Seeds
Prentinho-Heirloom Tobacco
Prentinho-Sustainable Seeds

Pretinho-Northwood Seeds
Prilep-Northwood Seeds
Prilep-Sustainable Seeds
Rapa Nui-B&T
Rapa Nui-JL Hudson
Reams 158-Northwood Seeds
Reams 158-Sustainable Seeds
Red Russia-Northwood Seeds
Red Russian-Daggawalla
Red Russian-New Hope
Red Russian-Northwood Seeds
Red Russian-Sustainable Seeds
Red Russian-Victory Seeds
Red Russian-West Seed Farm
Rose -Allies
Rose-B&T
Rose-Tobacum Rosa-Chiltern, UK
Rot Front-Northwood Seeds
Rot Front-Sustainable Seeds
Roulette-Chiltern, UK
Roulette-Nuts n Cones, UK
Rustica-Allies
Rustica-B&T
Rustica-Chiltern, UK
Rustica-Hardy Plants
Rustica-Impecta, Sweden
Rustica-Nicky's, UK
Rustica-Plant World Seeds, UK
Rustica-Rostliny-Semena, Czech
Rustica-Silene, Belgium
Rustica-The Tobacco Seed Co., UK
Rustica-Victory Seeds
Rustica-Virginia Tobacco Seeds, Spain
Rustica-Aztec-Horizon Herbs
Rustica-Aztec-Magic Garden Seeds

Rustica-Aztec-Sustainable Seeds
Rustica-Delaware Indian Sacred-Baker Creek
Rustica-Guarijio Makuchi-Native Seeds
Rustica-Hopi-B&T
Rustica-Hopi-Baker Creek
Rustica-Hopi-Heavenly Products
Rustica-Hopi-Horizon Herbs
Rustica-Hopi-Terroir Seeds
Rustica-Hopi-Terroir Seeds
Rustica-Hopi-Sustainable Seeds
Rustica-Hopley's-Special Plants, UK
Rustica-Indian-B&T
Rustica-Indian Black-Northwood Seeds
Rustica-Indian Black-Sustainable Seeds
Rustica-Indian Quadrivalvis-Chiltern, UK
Rustica-Isleta Pueblo-B&T
Rustica-Isleta Pueblo-Native Seeds
Rustica-Isleta Pueblo-Northwood Seeds
Rustica-Isleta Pueblo-The Tobacco Seed Co., UK
Rustica-Isleta Pueblo-Victory Seeds
Rustica-Kessu-Heirloom Tobacco
Rustica-Mapacho-Cibergarden, Spain
Rustica-Mapacho-Heavenly Products
Rustica-Mayan-Greta's
Rustica-Midewiwan Sacred-B&T
Rustica-Mohawk-Northwood Seeds
Rustica-Mohawk-Victory Seeds
Rustica-Mohawk-Sustainable Seeds
Rustica-Mopan Mayan-Heirloom Tobacco
Rustica-Mopan Mayan-Sustainable Seeds
Rustica-Mopan Myan-Northwood Seeds
Rustica Mountain Pima-Sustainable Seeds
Rustica-Mountain Pima-Native Seeds
Rustica-Mountain Pima-Northwood Seeds
Rustica-Mountain Pima-Victory Seeds

Rustica-Oneida-Heavenly Products
Rustica-Papante-B&T
Rustica-Papante-Native Seeds
Rustica-Punche-B&T
Rustica-Punche -Native Seeds
Rustica-Punche-Northwood Seeds
Rustica-Punche-Sustainable Seeds
Rustica-Sacred Cornplanter-Northwood Seeds
Rustica-Sacred Wyandot-Northwood Seeds
Rustica-San Juan-JL Hudson
Rustica-San Juan Pueblo-B&T
Rustica-Santo Domingo Ceremonial-Native Seeds
Rustica-Selsky-Semena-Osvia Slovakia
Rustica-Southern Tepehuan-Native Seeds
Rustica-Tarahumara El Cuervo-Native Seeds
Rustica-Tarahumara Wild-Native Seeds
Rustica-Oneida-Horizon Herbs
Sacred Cornplanter-Sustainable Seeds
Sacred Wyandot-Sustainable Seeds
Samsun-Cibergarden, Spain
Samsun-New Hope
Samsun-Victory Seeds
Samsun-Virginia Tobacco Seeds, Spain
Samsun-West Seed Farm
San Juan Pueblo-Adaptive Seeds
Saratoga Antique Shades-Seed Tapestry
Saratoga Appleblossom-Glacier Gardens (plants only)
Saratoga Appleblossom-Hardy Plants
Saratoga Appleblossom-Hazzard's Seed Store
Saratoga Appleblossom-Seed Tapestry
Saratoga Bicolor-Seed Tapestry
Saratoga Deep Rose-Glacier Gardens (plants only)
Saratoga Deep Rose-Richbar (plants only)
Saratoga Deep Rose-Seed Tapestry
Saratoga Deep Rose-Wasco (plants only)

Saratoga Lime-B&T
Saratoga Lime-Hazzard's Seed Store
Saratoga Lime-Richbar (plants only)
Saratoga Lime-Seed Tapestry
Saratoga Mixed-Hart's (plants only)
Saratoga Mixed-Hazzard's Seed Store
Saratoga Mixed-Seed Tapestry
Saratoga Mixed-Wasco (plants only)
Saratoga Purple-Seed Tapestry
Saratoga Purple Bicolor-Hart's (plants only)
Saratoga Purple Bicolor-Hazzard's Seed Store
Saratoga Red-Hart's (plants only)
Saratoga Red-Richbar (plants only)
Saratoga Red-Seed Tapestry
Saratoga Red Assorted-Glacier Gardens (plants only)
Saratoga Rose-Seed Tapestry
Saratoga White-Hart's (plants only)
Saratoga White-Seed Tapestry
Saratoga White-Wasco (plants only)
Sensation Mixed-B&T
Sensation Mixed-Baker Creek
Sensation Mixed-Chiltern, UK
Sensation Mixed -Dobies, UK
Sensation Mixed-Nuts n Cones, UK
Sensation Mixed-Seedaholic
Sensation Mixed-Thompson & Morgan, US & UK
Sherazi-Sustainable Seeds
Shirazi-Adaptive Seeds
Shirazi-Allies
Shirazi-Daggawalla
Shirazi-Heirloom Tobacco
Shirazi-New Hope
Shirazi-Northwood Seeds
Shirazi-Virginia Tobacco Seeds, Spain
Shirey-B&T

Shirey-JL Hudson
Shirey-Northwood Seeds
Shirey-The Tobacco Seed Co., UK
Shirey-Virginia Tobacco Seeds, Spain
Shirey-West Seed Farm
Shirey-Sustainable Seeds
Silk Leaf-New Hope
Silk Leaf-Northwood Seeds
Silk Leaf-West Seed Farm
Silk Leaf-Sustainable Seeds
Silver River-Northwood Seeds
Silver River-Sustainable Seeds
Simon-Northwood Seeds
Simox-Sustainable Seeds
Small Stalk Black Mammoth-B&T
Small Stalk Black Mammoth-Daggawalla
Small Stalk Black Mammoth-JL Hudson
Small Stalk Black Mammoth-Northwood Seeds
Small Stalk Black Mammoth-Virginia Tobacco Seeds, Spain
Small Stalk Black Mammoth-Sustainable Seeds
Sobolchskii-Sustainable Seeds
Sobolchskii193-Northwood Seeds
Southern Beauty-New Hope
Southern Beauty-Northwood Seeds
Southern Beauty -Sustainable Seeds
Southern Beauty-The Tobacco Seed Co., UK
Southern Beauty-West Seed Farm
Spectrum-Northwood Seeds
Spectrum-Sustainable Seeds
Stag Horn-Northwood Seeds
Stag Horn-Sustainable Seeds
Stag Horn-The Tobacco Seed Co., UK
Stolac 17-Northwood Seeds
Stolac 17-Sustainable Seeds
Suaveolens-Crocus

Suaveolens-De Werkplaats, Netherlands
Suaveolens-Notcutts
Suaveolens-Seedman.com (UK only)
Suaveolens-Thompson & Morgan, US & UK
Sumatra-Florida-Sustainable Seeds
Sumatra-Florida-Victory Seeds
Sylvestris-Allies
Sylvestris-B&T
Sylvestris-Botanical Interests
Sylvestris-Chiltern, UK
Sylvestris-Crocus
Sylvestris-D T Brown, UK
Sylvestris-De Werkplaats Netherlands
Sylvestris-Diane's
Sylvestris-Diane's Seeds
Sylvestris-Hardy Plants
Sylvestris-Hazzard's Seed Store
Sylvestris-Heavenly Products
Sylvestris -Impecta, Sweden
Sylvestris-JL Hudson
Sylvestris-New Hope
Sylvestris-Nicky's, UK
Sylvestris-Northwood Seeds
Sylvestris-Northwood Seeds
Sylvestris-Notcutts
Sylvestris-Nuts n Cones, UK
Sylvestris-Plant World Seeds, UK
Sylvestris-Portland Nursery (plants only)
Sylvestris-Sarah Raven, UK
Sylvestris-Seedaholic
Sylvestris-Seedman.com (UK only)
Sylvestris-Seeds of Eaden
Sylvestris-Select Seeds
Sylvestris-Silene, Belgium
Sylvestris-Special Plants, UK

Sylvestris-Swallowtail
Sylvestris-Terroir Seeds
Sylvestris-Terroir Seeds
Sylvestris-The Flower Company (plants only)
Sylvestris-The Tobacco Seed Co., UK
Sylvestris-Thompson & Morgan, US & UK
Sylvestris-Von Trapp Greenhouse (plants only)
Sylvestris-White Flower Farms (plants only)
Sylvestris-Only the Lonely-Sustainable Seeds
Symbol 14-Northwood Seeds
Tasoua-Virginia Tobacco Seeds, Spain
Tasoua-Sustainable Seeds
Tasova-Northwood Seeds
Tekne-Northwood Seeds
Tekne-Sustainable Seeds
Tennessee Red-Sustainable Seeds
Thailand-Northwood Seeds
Thailand-Sustainable Seeds
Thompson-Northwood Seeds
Thompson-Sustainable Seeds
Tinkerbell-B&T
Tinkerbell-De Werkplaats, Netherlands
Tinkerbell-Nuts n Cones, UK
Tinkerbell-Plant World Seeds, UK
Tinkerbell-Portland Nursery (plants only)
Tinkerbell-Silene, Belgium
Tinkerbell-Special Plants, UK
Tinkerbell-Swallowtail
TN 86 LC-Sustainable Seeds
TN 90 LC -Sustainable Seeds
Tobacco Colorado-Northwood Seeds
Tree-Heavenly Products
Tree-Impecta, Sweden
Tree-Magic Gardens Seeds
Tree-Blue Tree Glauca-The Tobacco Seed Co, UK

Tree-Glauca-B&T
Tree-Glauca-Chiltern, UK
Tree-Glauca-Daggawalla
Tree-Glauca-Heirloom Tobacco
Tree-Glauca-JL Hudson
Tree-Glauca-Virginia Tobacco Seeds, Spain
Tree-Salamenia Blue-The Tobacco Seed Co., UK
Tree-Glauca-Allies
Turtlefoot-The Tobacco Seed Co., UK
Vavilov-Northwood Seeds
Vavilov-Sustainable Seeds
Vesta 64-Northwood Seeds
Vesta 64-Sustainable Seeds
Virginia-Heirloom Tobacco
Virginia-Impecta, Sweden
Virginia 116-Northwood Seeds
Virginia 116-Sustainable Seeds
Virginia 509-Sustainable Seeds
Virginia Bright-Victory Seeds
Virginia Bright Leaf-New Hope
Virginia Gold-Cibergarden, Spain
Virginia Gold-Daggawalla
Virginia Gold-Organica
Virginia Gold-The Tobacco Seed Co., UK
Virginia Gold-Virginia Tobacco Seeds, Spain
Virginia-Spanish-Virginia Tobacco Seeds, Spain
Virginia VA 309-B&T
Virginia VA 309-JL Hudson
Vuelta Abajo-Heirloom Tobacco
Vuelta Abajo-Northwood Seeds
Vuelta Abajo-Sustainable Seeds
Walker's Broadleaf-B&T
Walker's Broadleaf-JL Hudson
Walker's Broadleaf-Northwood Seeds
Walker's Broadleaf-Organica

Walker's Broadleaf-Sustainable Seeds
Warner-New Hope
Warner-West Seed Farm
Whisper Mixed-Moles Seeds, UK
Whisper Mixed-Nuts n Cones, UK
Whisper Mixed-Portland Nursery (plants only)
Whisper Mixed-Sarah Raven, UK
Whisper Mixed-Seeds of Eaden
Whisper Mixed-Thompson & Morgan, US & UK
Whisper Mixes-Silene, Belgium
White Mammoth-New Hope
White Mammoth-Sustainable Seeds
White Stem Orinoco-New Hope
Wisconsin 901-Northwood Seeds
Wisconsin 901-Sustainable Seeds
Wisconsin Seedleaf-New Hope
Xanthy-Northwood Seeds
Xanthy-Sustainable Seeds
Yellow Leaf-Northwood Seeds
Yellow Leaf-Sustainable Seeds
Yellow Orinoco-West Seed Farm
Yellow Oronoko-Sustainable Seeds
Yellow Prior-New Hope
Yellow Prior-Northwood Seeds
Yellow Prior-Sustainable Seeds
Yellow Prior-The Tobacco Seed Co., UK
Yellow Prior-West Seed Farm
Yellow Twist Bud-Sustainable Seeds
Yenidge-Heirloom Tobacco
Yenidje-Northwood Seeds
Yenidje-Sustainable Seeds
Yumbo-Heirloom Tobacco
Yumbo-Northwood Seeds
Yumbo-Sustainable Seeds
Zimmer Spanish-New Hope
Zimmer Spanish-West Seed Farm

Appendix C

SYNONYMS OF COMMON NAMES
OF FEATURED VARIETIES

Only the Lonely. *See* Sylvestris
Ox Tongue. *See* One Sucker
Peach Screamer. *See* Glutinosa
Persian Lime Green. *See* Lime Green
Persian Tobacco. *See* Affinis. *See* Affinis
Quadrivalvis. *See* Indian
Samsun tobacco. *See* Black Sea Samsun
San Juan Tree. *See* Tree
Shadeleaf. *See*
Solaniflora. *See* Cimarron
South American tobacco. *See* Sylvestris
Sweet Scented. *See* Jasmine
Tabaco Silvestre. *See* Acuminata
TN 86. *See* Burley
TN 90. *See* Burley
TND 950. *See* Burley
Tobaco de Cerro. *See* Acuminata
Tom Ross Madole. *See* Madole
Tongue tobacco. *See* One Sucker
Trigonophylla. *See* Desert
Turkish Basma. *See* Basma
Turkish Izmir. *See* Izmir
Virginia 509. *See* Burley
Virginia Brightleaf. *See* Virginia
Virginia Brown Leaf. *See* Brown Leaf
Virginia Cigarette. *See* Virginia
Virginia Gold. *See* Virginia
Virginia Smoking. *See* Virginia

Warner. *See* Burley
White Mammoth. *See* Mammoth
White Stem Orinoco. *See* Orinoco
Woodland tobacco. *See* Sylvestris
Wrapper. *See* Connecticut Tobaccos
Yellow Mammoth. *See* Mammoth
Yellow Orinoco. *See* Orinoco
Yellow Twist Bud. *See* Burley

A p p e n d i x   D

COMPREHENSIVE LIST OF COMMON NAMES

This is a compilation of tobacco types culled from many sources. They may no longer be available, nor have they been verified. The list is for readers who are interested in historical research.

Common Name   Binominal Name

Aboriginal (Australia), *nicotiana excelsior*
Acaulis, *nicotiana acaulis*
Acuminata, *nicotiana acuminata*
African (Nambia), *nicotiana africana*
African Red, *nicotiana tabacum african red*
Alamena Blue, *nicotiana glauca*
Ameghinoi (Argentina), *nicotiana ameghinoi*
Amplexicaulis (Australia), *nicotiana amplexicaulis*
Andean Mapacho, *nicotiana rustica mapacho*
Antennaria, *nicotiana antennaria*
Arentsii (Boliva), *nicotiana arentsii*
Argentine, *nicotiana sylvestris*
Ash (type 41), *nicotiana tabacum Ash (type 41)*
Atkin's Madole, *nicotiana tabacum atkin's madole*
Australian, *nicotiana suaveolens*
Australian Coast, *nicotiana maritima*
Avalon Appleblossom, *nicotiana sanderae f1 avalon appleblossom*

Avalon Bright Pink, *nicotiana sanderae f1 Avalon Bright Pink*
Avalon Burgundy, *nicotiana sanderae f1 avalon burgundy*
Avalon Lime, *nicotiana sanderae f1 avalon lime*
Avalon Lime and Purple, *nicotiana sanderae f1 avalon lime and purple*
Avalon Mixed Dwarf, *nicotiana sanderae f1 avalon mixed dwarf*
Avalon Peach, *nicotiana sanderae f1 avalon peach*
Avalon Pink Picotee, *nicotiana sanderae f1 avalon pink picotee*
Avalon Red, *nicotiana sanderae f1 avalon red*
Avalon Salmon, *nicotiana sanderae f1 avalon salmon*
Avalon White, *nicotiana sanderae f1 avalon white*
Azambujae (Brazil), *nicotiana azambujae*
Aztec, *nicotiana rustica aztec*
Baby Bella or Babybella Antique Red hybrid, *nicotiana sanderae f1 baby bella*
Bafra, *nicotiana tabacum bafra*
Baiano (Hungarian type), *nicotiana tabacum baiano*
Bamboo Shoot, *nicotiana tabacum bamboo shoot*
Banana Leaf, *nicotiana tabacum banana leaf*
Barinas (Venezuala), *nicotiana tabacum barinas*
Barnett Special, *nicotiana tabacum barnett special*
Basma (Turkey), *nicotiana tabacum basma*
Baur, *nicotiana tabacum Baur*
Benavidesii (Peru), *nicotiana benavidesii*
Benthamiana (Australia), *nicotiana benthamiana*
Big Gem, *nicotiana tabacum big gem*
Bigelovii, *nicotiana bigelovii*
Big Love, *nicotiana bigelovii*
Bitlis, *nicotiana tabacum bitlis*
Black Mammoth, *nicotiana tabacum black mammoth*
Black Sea Basma, *nicotiana tabacum basma*
Black Sea Samsun, *nicotiana tabacum samsun*
Blanco, *nicotiana tabacum blanco*
Blue Tree Glauca, *nicotiana glauca*
Bonanza, *nicotiana tabacum bonanza*
Bonariensis (Uruguay), *nicotiana bonariensis*

Bosikappal (India), *Nicotiana bosikappal*
Brazilian Tree, *Nicotiana tomentosa*
Brown Leaf, *nicotiana tabacum brown leaf virginia*
Bugle Call Yellow, *nicotiana glauca*
Burbidgeae (Australia), *nicotiana burbidgeae*
Burley 21, *nicotiana tabacum*
Burley 37, *nicotiana tabacum burley 37*
Burley 49, *nicotiana tabacum burley 49*
Burley 64, *nicotiana tabacum burley 64*
Burley BH04P LC Hybrid, *nicotiana tabacum burley hybrid bh04p lc*
Burley Clay's 403 LC Hybrid, *nicotiana tabacum burley hybrid clay's 403 LC*
Burley Co-op 313 Hybrid, *nicotiana tabacum burley hybrid co-op 313*
Burley Co-op 543 Hybrid, *nicotiana tabacum burley hybrid co-op 543*
Burley Gold Dollar, *nicotiana tabacum gold dollar*
Burley HB 3307 LC Hybrid, *nicotiana tabacum burley hybrid hb 3307 lc*
Burley Hybrid 402, *nicotiana tabacum burley hybrid 402*
Burley Hybrid 403LC, *nicotiana tabacum burley hybrid 403lc*
Burley Hybrid 501LC, *nicotiana tabacum burley hybrid 501lc*
Burley Hybrid 502, *nicotiana tabacum burley hybrid 502*
Burley KT 200 LC Hybrid, *Nicotiana tabacum burley hybrid kt 200 lc*
Burley KT 204 LC Hybrid, *nicotiana tabacum burley hybrid kt 204 lc*
Burley KT 204 LC Hybrid, *nicotiana tabacum burley hybrid kt 200 lc*
Burley KT 206 LC Hybrid, *nicotiana tabacum burley hybrid kt 206 lc*
Burley KT 209 LC Hybrid, *nicotiana tabacum burley hybrid kt 209 lc*
Burley KT 210 LC Hybrid, *nicotiana tabacum burley hybrid kt 210 lc*
Burley KT 212 LC Hybrid, *nicotiana tabacum hybrid kt 212 lc*
Burley KY 10, *nicotiana tabacum burley ky 10*
Burley KY 12, *nicotiana tabacum burley ky 12*
Burley KY 14, *nicotiana tabacum burley ky 14*
Burley KY 14LC Hybrid, *nicotiana tabacum burley hybrid ky 14lc*
Burley KY 14XL8 LC Hybrid, *nicotiana tabacum burley hybrid ky 200lc*
Burley KY 15, *nicotiana tabacum burley ky 15*
Burley KY 17, *nicotiana tabacum burley ky 17*
Burley KY 17LC Hybrid, *nicotiana tabacum burley Hybrid ky17lc*

Burley KY 190, *nicotiana tabacum ky 190*
Burley KY 21, *nicotiana tabacum burley ky 21*
Burley KY 5, *nicotiana tabacum burley ky 5*
Burley KY 8959, *nicotiana tabacum burley ky 8959*
Burley KY 9, *nicotiana tabacum burley ky 9*
Burley KY 907, *nicotiana tabacum ky 907*
Burley KY 908, *nicotiana tabacum burley ky 908*
Burley KY 910 Hybrid, *nicotiana tabacum burley ky 910*
Burley KY10, *nicotiana tabacum burley ky 10*
Burley MS 21 x 14 Hybrid, *nicotiana tabacum burley hybrid ms 21 x 14*
Burley MS 21 x L8 Hybrid, *nicotiana tabacum burley hybrid ms 21 x L8*
Burley MS 21 x12 Hybrid, *nicotiana tabacum burley hybrid ms 21 x 12*
Burley MS 21x 10 Hybrid, *nicotiana tabacum burley hybrid ms 21 x 10*
Burley ms 21x10 Hybrid, *nicotiana tabacum burley ms 21x10 hybrid*
Burley MS 21x9 Hybrid, *Nicotiana tabacum burley hybrid ms 21 x 9*
Burley MS 37 x L8 Hybrid, *nicotiana tabacum burley hybrid ms 37 x l8*
Burley MS KY 10 x L8 Hybrid, *nicotiana tabacum burley Hybrid ms ky 10 x l8*
Burley MS KY 12 x L8 Hybrid, *nicotiana tabacum burley Hybrid ms 12 x L8*
Burley MS KY 14 x Burley 64 Hybrid, *nicotiana tabacum burley Hybrid ms ky 14 x 64*
Burley ms KY14xL8 Hybrid, *Nicotiana tabacum burley ms ky 14xl8 hybrid*
Burley ms R 7-12 Hybrid, *nicotiana tabacum burley ms r 7-12 hybrid*
Burley N 126 Hybrid, *nicotiana tabacum burley hybrid n126*
Burley N 7371 Hybrid, *nicotiana tabacum burley hybrid n 7371*
Burley N 7371 LC Hybrid, *Nicotiana tabacum burley hybrid n 7371 lc*
Burley N 77 Hybrid, *nicotiana tabacum burley hybrid n 77*
Burley N 777Hybrid, *nicotiana tabacum burley hybrid n 777*
Burley N 88 Hybrid, *nicotiana tabacum burley hybrid n 88*
Burley NBH 98 Hybrid, *nicotiana tabacum burley hybrid nbh 98*
Burley NBH 98 Hybrid, *nicotiana tabacum burley hybrid nbh 98*
Burley NC 2, *nicotiana tabacum burley nc 2*
Burley NC 2000, *nicotiana tabacum burley nc 2000*
Burley NC 2002, *nicotiana tabacum burley nc 2002*

Burley NC 3, *nicotiana tabacum burley*
nc 3
Burley NC 4, *nicotiana tabacum burley nc4*
Burley NC 5, *nicotiana tabacum burley nc 5*
Burley NC 5, *nicotiana tabacum burley nc 5*
Burley NC 6, *nicotiana tabacum burley nc 6*
Burley NC 7, *nicotiana tabacum burley nc 7*
Burley NC BH 129 Hybrid, *nicotiana tabacum burley hybrid nc bh 129*
Burley NCBH 129 Hybrid, *nicotiana tabacum burley hybrid nc bh 129*
Burley PF-561 Hybrid, *nicotiana tabacum burley hybrid pf-561*
Burley R 610LC Hybrid, *nicotiana tabacum burley hybrid hybrid r 610 lc*
Burley R 611 Hybrid, *nicotiana tabacum burley hybrid r 611*
Burley R 630 LC Hybrid, *nicotiana tabacum burley hybrid r 630 lc*
Burley R 630LC Hybrid, *nicotiana tabacum burley hybrid r 630 lc*
Burley R 712 LC Hybrid, *nicotiana tabacum burley hybrid r 712 lc*
Burley R 800 Hybrid, *nicotiana tabacum burley hybrid r 800*
Burley R-141 Hybrid, *nicotiana tabacum burley hybrid r-141*
Burley R7-11 Hybrid, *nicotiana tabacum burley hybrid r7-11*
Burley R7-12LC Hybrid, *nicotiana tabacum burley hybrid r7-12lc*
Burley TA 14 Common Smoking, *nicotiana tabacum burley T14 common smoking*
Burley TA 42 KY 8959 Hybrid, *nicotiana tabacum burley Hybrid ta 2 ky 8959*
Burley TA 44 NC 2 Hybrid, *nicotiana tabacum burley hybrid ta 44 nc 2*
Burley TA 46 VA 509 Hybrid, *nicotiana tabacum burley hybrid TA 46 VA 509*
Burley TA MS21 Hybrid, *nicotiana tabacum burley hybrid ta ms21*
Burley TA51 NC BH129 Hybrid, *nicotiana tabacum burley hybrid ta51 nc bh129*
Burley TN 86, *nicotiana tabacum burley tn 86*
Burley TN 86 LC Hybrid, *nicotiana tabacum burley hybrid tn 86 lc*
Burley TN 90 LC Hybrid, *nicotiana tabacum burley hybrid hybrid tn 90 LC*
Burley TN 97 Hybrid, *nicotiana tabacum burley hybrid tn 97*
Burley TN 97 LC Hybrid, *nicotiana tabacum burley hybrid tn 97 lc*

Burley TN90, *nicotiana tabacum burley tn 90*
Burley VA 509, *nicotiana tabacum burley va 509*
Burley VA 510, *nicotiana tabacum burley va 510*
Burley VA 528, *nicotiana tabacum burley va 528*
Catterton, *nicotiana tabacum catterton*
Cavicola (Australia), *nicotiana cavicola*
CC 65 Hybrid, *nicotiana tabacum hybrid cc 65*
CC 67 Hybrid, *nicotiana tabacum hybrid cc 67*
CC 700 Hybrid, *nicotiana tabacum hybrid cc700*
CC13 Hybrid, *nicotiana tabacum hybrid cc13*
CC27 Hybrid, *nicotiana tabacum hybrid cc27*
CC33 Hybrid, *nicotiana tabacum hybrid cc33*
CC35 Hybrid, *nicotiana tabacum hybrid cc35*
CC37 Hybrid, *nicotiana tabacum hybrid cc37*
Certified Madole, *nicotiana tabacum madole*
Cherry Red, *nicotiana tabacum cherry red*
Cherry Red 401, *nicotiana tabacum cherry red 401*
Chilean, *nicotiana langsdorfii*
Cimarron, *nicotiana solanifolia*
Clevelands (USA-SW), *nicotinan clevelandii*
Coast (Australia), *nicotiana maritima*
Coker 176 Hybrid, *nicotiana tabacum hybrid coker 176*
Coker 319 Hybrid, *nicotiana tabacum hybrid coker 319*
Coker 371 Gold Hybrid, *nicotiana tabacum hybrid coker 371 gold*
Coker 371 Gold Hybrid, *nicotiana tabacum hybrid coker 371 gold*
Coker 48 Hybrid, *nicotiana tabacum hybrid coker 48*
Comstock Spanish, *nicotiana tabacum comstock Spanish*
Connecticut Broadleaf, *nicotiana tabacum connecticut broadleaf*
Cordifolia (Chile), *nicotiana cordifolia*
Corymbosa (Chile), *nicotiana corymbosa*
Costello Negro, *nicotiana tabacum costello negro*
Coyote, *nicotiana attenuata*
Cream Splash, *nicotiana langsdorfii cream splash*
Crimson Bedder, *nicotiana alata sanderae f1 crimson bedder*
Criollo (Cuba), *nicotiana tabacum criollo*

Criollo 98, *nicotiana tabacum criollo 98*
CU 1097 Hybrid, *nicotiana tabacum hybrid cu 1097*
CU 165 Hybrid, *nicotiana tabacum hybrid cu 165*
CU 263 Hybrid, *nicotiana tabacum hybrid cu 263*
CU 468 Hybrid, *nicotiana tabacum hybrid cu 486*
CU 561 Hybrid, *nicotiana tabacum hybrid cu 561*
Cuba 4, *nicotiana cuba 4*
Dark KY 171, *nicotiana tabacum dark ky-171*
Dark TND 950, *nicotiana tabacum dark TND-950*
Daule (Ecuador), *nicotiana daule*
Debneyi (Australia), *nicotiana debneyi*
Delgold, *nicotiana tabacum delgold*
Desert obtusifolia, *nicotiana obtusifolia*
Desert trigonophylla, *nicotiana trigonophylla*
DF 300 Hybrid, *nicotiana tabacum hybrid df 300*
DF 485 Hybrid, *nicotiana tabacum hybrid df 485*
DF 911 Hybrid, *nicotiana tabacum hybrid df 911*
Dixie Bright 27, *Nicotiana tabacum dixie bright 27*
Dixie Shade, *Nicotiana tabacum dixie shade*
Domino Antique Peach, *nicotiana sanderae f1 domino antique peach*
Domino Antique Red, *nicotiana sanderae f1 domino antique red*
Domino Antique Shades, *nicotiana sanderae f1 domino antiqe shades*
Domino Crimson, *nicotiana sanderae f1 domino crimson*
Domino Light Purple, *nicotiana sanderae f1 domino light purple*
Domino Lime Green, *nicotiana sanderae f1 domino lime green*
Domino Mixed, *nicotiana sanderae f1 domino mixed*
Domino Pink White Eye, *nicotiana sanderae f1 domino pink white eye*
Domino Purple, *nicotiana sanderae f1 domino purple*
Domino Purple White Eye, *nicotiana sanderae f1 domino purple white eye*
Domino Red, *nicotiana sanderae f1 domino red*
Domino Rose Picotee, *nicotiana sanderae f1 domino rose picotee*
Domino Salmon pink, *nicotiana sanderae domino salmon pink*
Domino White, *nicotiana sanderae f1 domino white*
Downy, *nicotiana tomentosa*
DT 508 Hybrid, *nicotiana tabacum hybrid dt 508*

DT 518 Hybrid, *nicotiana tabacum hybrid DT 518*
DT 538 LC Hybrid, *nicotiana tabacum hybrid dt 538 lc*
DT 592 Hybrid, *nicotiana tabacum hybrid dt 592*
Dwarf White Bedder, *nicotiana alata sanderae f1 dwarf white bedder*
Easter Island, *nicotiana rustica rapa nui*
Erzegovina Lecce, *nicotiana tabacum erzegovian lecce*
Eschly #1 (type 41) Hybrid, *nicotiana tabacum eschly #1 (type 41)*
Exigua (Australia), *nicotiana exigua*
Fiddleleaf, *nicotiana repanda*
Florida Sumatra, *nicotiana tabacum florida sumatra*
Flowering, *nicotiana mutabilis*
Flue Cured NC100 Hybrid, *nicotiana tabacum hybrid nc100*
Flue Cured NC71 Hybrid, *nicotiana tabacum hybrid nc 71*
Flue Cured NC72 Hybrid, *nicotiana tabacum hybrid nc72*
Flue Cured PVH03 Hybrid, *nicotiana tabacum hybrid pvh03*
Flue Cured PVH09 Hybrid, *nicotiana tabacum hybrid pvh309*
Foreheimer Gundertheimes III Hybrid, *nicotiana tobaccum hybrid foreheimer gundertheimes III*
Forgetiana (Brazil), *Nicotiana forgetiana*
Fragans (French Polynesia), *nicotiana fragrans*
Fragrant Cloud, *nicotiana sanderae f1 fragrant cloud*
Fragrant Delight, *nicotiana sanderae f1 fragrant delight*
GF 318 Hybrid, *nicotiana tabacum hybrid gf 318*
GL 318 Hybrid, *nicotiana tabacum hybrid gl 318*
GL 330 Hybrid, *nicotiana tabacum hybrid gl 330*
GL 338 Hybrid, *nicotiana tabacum hybrid gl 338*
GL 350 Hybrid, *nicotiana tabacum hybrid gl 350*
GL 368 Hybrid, *nicotiana tabacum hybrid gl 338*
GL 395 Hybrid, *nicotiana tabacum hybrid gl 395*
GL 737 Hybrid, *nicotiana tabacum hybrid gl 737*
GL 939 Hybrid, *nicotiana tabacum hybrid gl 939*
GL 973 Hybrid, *nicotiana tabacum hybrid gl 973*
Glauca (USA-SW), *nicotiana glauca*
Glessnor or Glessner, *Nicotiana tabacum glessnor*

Glutinosa, *Nicotiana glutinosa*
Gold Dollar, *nicotiana tabacum gold dollar*
Gold Seal Special TA 101 Hybrid, *nicotiana tabacum hybrid gold seal special ta 101*
Golden Burley, *nicotiana tabacum golden burley*
Goldleaf Orinoco (Peru), *nicotiana tabacum goldleaf orinoco*
Goodspedii (Australia), *nicotiana goodspedii*
Goose Creek Red, *nicotiana tabacum goose creek red*
Gossei (Australia), *nicotiana gossei*
Green Brior (Burley), *nicotiana tabacum green brior*
Greenwood, *nicotiana tabacum green wood*
Habano (Honduras), *nicotiana tabacum habano*
Harrow Velvet (Burley), *nicotiana tabacum harrow velvet*
Haskovo, *nicotiana tabacum haskovo*
Havana 142, *nicotiana tabacum havana 142*
Havana 211, *nicotiana tabacum havana 211*
Havana 263, *nicotiana tabacum havana 263*
Havana 307, *nicotiana tabacum havana 307*
Havana 322, *nicotiana tabacum Havana 322*
Havana 38, *nicotiana tabacum havana 38*
Havana 501, *nicotiana tabacum havana 501*
Havana 503, *nicotiana tabacum havana 503*
Havana 503B, *nicotiana tabacum havana 503B*
Havana 608, *nicotiana tabacum havana 608*
Havana 615, *nicotiana tabacum havana 615*
Havana Appleblossom, *nicotiana sanderae f1 havana appleblossom*
Havana Carmine Rose, *nicotiana sanderae f1 havana carmine Rose*
Havana Lilac Rose, *nicotiana sanderae f1 havana lilac rose*
Havana Lime, *nicotiana sanderae f1 havana lime*
Havana Mixed, *nicotiana sanderae f1 havana mixed*
Havana Purple, *nicotiana sanderae f1 havana purple*
Havana Red, *nicotiana sanderae f1 havana red*
Havana True Lime, *nicotiana sanderae f1 havana true lime*
Havana White, *nicotiana sanderae f1 havana white*

Hawkwind, *nicotiana rustica hawkwind*
HB Old Narrowleaf (type 41), *nicotiana tabacum HB old narrowleaf (type 41)*
Head's Madole, *nicotiana tabacum head's madole*
Heaven Scent, *nicotiana sanderae f1 heaven scent*
Hesperis (Australia), *nicotiana hesperis*
Heterantha (Australia), *nicotiana heterantha*
Hickory Prior, *nicotiana tabacum hickory prior*
Hopi, *nicotiana rustica hopi*
Hopley's, *nicotiana rustica hopleys*
Hot Chocolate, *nicotiana hot chocolate*
Improved Narrow Leaf (type 41), *nicotiana tabacum improved narrow leaf (type 41)*
Indian, *nicotiana bigelovii*
Indian, *nicotiana rustica*
Ingulba (Australia), *nicotiana ingulba*
Isleta Pueblo, *nicotiana rustica isleta pueblo*
Izmir Lebanese, *nicotiana tabacum izmir lebanese*
Izmir Ozbis, *nicotiana tabacum ozbis*
Jasmine, *nicotiana alata var. grandiflora or nicotiana affinis var. grandiflora*
Jernigan's Madole Hybrid, *nicotiana tabacum jerigan's madole*
K 149 Hybrid, *nicotiana tabacum hybrid k 149*
K 326 Hybrid, *nicotiana tabacum hybrid k 326*
K 346 Hybrid, *nicotiana tabacum hybrid k 346*
K 358 Hybrid, *nicotiana tabacum hybrid k 358*
K 394 Hybrid, *nicotiana tabacum hybrid k 394*
K 399 Hybrid, *nicotiana tabacum hybrid k 399*
K 730 Hybrid, *nicotiana tabacum hybrid k 730*
Kawakamii (Bolivia), *nicotiana kawakamii*
Keller, *nicotiana tabacum keller*
Kelly Brownleaf Burley, *nicotiana tabacum burley kelly brownleaf*
Kelly Burley, *nicotiana tabacum burley kelly*
Kesu or Kess, *nicotiana rustica kessu*
Knightana, *nicotiana knightiana*

KT D4 LC Hybrid, *nicotiana tabacum hybrid kt d6 lc*
KT D6 LC Hybrid, *Nicotiana tabacum hybrid kt d6 lc*
KT-D8 LC Hybrid, *nicotiana tabacum hybrid kt d8 lc*
Kumanovo, *nicotiana tabacum kumanovo*
KY 151, *nicotiana tabacum ky 151*
KY 160, *nicotiana tabacum ky 160*
KY 171, *nicotiana tabacum ky 171*
KY 171 LC, *nicotiana tabacum hybrid ky 171*
Lancaster Seed Leaf, *Nicotiana tabacum lancaster seed leaf*
Langsdorfii, *nicotiana langsdorfii*
Lemon Tree, *nicotiana langsdorfii*
Linearis (Chile), *nicotiana linearis*
Little Crittenden, *nicotiana tabacum little crittenden*
Little Dutch (Germany), *nicotiana tabacum little dutch*
Little Wood, *nicotiana tabacum little wood*
Lizard Tail Orinoco, *nicotiana tabacum lizard tail orinoco*
Lizard Tail turtle foot, *nicotiana tabacum lizard tail orinoco x turtle foot*
Long Flower or Longflower (Australia), *nicotiana longiflora*
Long Red, *nicotiana tabacum long red*
Longibracteata (Chile), *nicotiana longibracteata*
Mack (type 41) Hybrid, *nicotiana tabacum mack (type 41)*
Madole, *nicotiana tabacum madole*
Madole improved, *nicotiana tabacum madole improved*
Madole narrow leaf, *nicotiana tabacum madole narrow leaf*
Madole Tom Ross, *nicotiana tabacum madole tom ross*
Mammoth TA28, *nicotiana tabacum mammoth TA 28*
Mammoth White, *nicotiana tabacum mammoth white*
Manyflower, *nicotiana acuminata*
Mapacho, *nicotiana rustica mapacho*
Maritima, *nicotiana maritima*
Marshmallow, *nicotiana mutabilis*
Maryland 10, *nicotiana tabacum maryland 10*
Maryland 14 D2, *nicotiana tabacum maryland 14 D2*
Maryland 21, *nicotiana tabacum maryland 21*
Maryland 40, *nicotiana tabacum maryland 40*

Maryland 59, *nicotiana tabacum maryland 59*
Maryland 64, *nicotiana tabacum maryland 64*
McNair 135 Hybrid, *nicotiana tabacum hybrid mc nair 135*
McNair 373 Hybrid, *nicotiana tabacum hybrid mcnair 373*
McNair 944 Hybrid, *nicotiana tabacum hybrid mcnair 944*
MD A30 (Chatterton), *nicotiana tabacum MD A30*
Megalosiphon (Australia), *nicotiana megalosiphon*
Merlin Magic, *nicotiana sanderare f1 merlin magic*
Midewivan, *nicotiana rustica midewiwan sacred*
Miersii (Chile), *nicotiana miersii*
Mohawk, *nicotiana rustica mohawk*
Monte Calme, *nicotiana tabacum monte calme*
Monte Calme Blonde, *nicotiana tabacum monte calme blonde*
Monte Calme Brun, *nicotiana tabacum monte calme brun*
Monte Calme Yellow, *nicotiana tabacum monte calme yellow*
Mop Cap, *nicotiana rustica mop cap*
Mopan Maya, *nicotiana rustica mopan*
Mountain Pima, *nicotiana rustica mountain pima*
Mustard Tree, *nicotiana glauca*
Mustcatelle, *nicotiana tabacum muscatelle*
Mutablis (Brazil), *nicotiana mutablis*
Native (Australia), *nicotiana occidentalis*
NC 100 Hybrid, *nicotiana tabacum hybrid NC 100*
NC 102 Hybrid, *nicotiana tabacum hybrid NC 102*
NC 196 Hybrid, *nicotiana tabacum hybrid nc 196*
NC 2326 Hybrid, *nicotiana tabacum hybrid nc 2326*
NC 27NF Hybrid, *nicotiana tabacum hybrid nc 27 nf*
NC 291 Hybrid, *nicotiana tabacum hybrid nc 291*
NC 297 Hybrid, *nicotiana tabacum hybrid nc 297*
NC 299 Hybrid, *nicotiana tabacum hybrid nc 299*
NC 37NF Hybrid, *nicotiana tabacum hybrid nc 37NF*
NC 471 Hybrid, *nicotiana tabacum hybrid nc 471*
NC 55 Hybrid, *nicotiana tabacum hybrid nc 55*
NC 567 Hybrid, *nicotiana tabacum hybrid nc 567*
NC 60 Hybrid, *nicotiana tabacum hybrid nc 60*

NC 606 Hybrid, *nicotiana tabacum hybrid nc 606*
NC 71 Hybrid, *nicotiana tabacum hybrid nc 71*
NC 72 Hybrid, *nicotiana tabacum hybrid nc 72*
NC 79 Hybrid, *nicotiana tabacum hybrid nc 79*
NC 810 Hybrid, *nicotiana tabacum hybrid nc 810*
NC 82 Hybrid, *nicotiana tabacum hybrid nc 82*
NC 92 Hybrid, *nicotiana tabacum hybrid nc 92*
NC 95 Hybrid, *nicotiana tabacum hybrid nc 95*
NC TG 100 Hybrid, *nicotiana tabacum hybrid nc tg 97*
NC TG 97 Hybrid, *nicotiana tabacum hybrid nc tg 97*
Nesophila, *nicotiana nesophilia*
Nicki Lime, *Nicotiana f1 hybrid nicki lime*
Nicki Mixed, *nicotiana f1 hybrid nicki mixed*
Nicki Red, *nicotiana fi hybrid nicki red*
Nicki Rose, *nicotiana fi hybrid nicki rose*
Nicki White, *nicotiana fi hybrid nicki white*
Nikki Lime, *nicotiana alata nikki lime*
Nikki Mixed, *nicotiana alata nikki mixed*
Nikki Red, *nicotiana alata nikki red*
Nikki Rose, *nicotiana alata nikki rose*
Nudicaulis (Mexico), *nicotiana nudicaulis*
Ohio Dutch, *nicotiana tabacum ohio dutch*
One Sucker KY-165, *nicotiana tabacum one sucker ky-165*
One Sucker Variety OS 400,
Oneida, *nicotiana rustica oneida*
Only the Lonely, *nicotiana sylvestris*
Orinoco, *nicotiana tabacum orinoco*
Orinoco TA 05, *nicotiana tabacum TA 05*
Otophora (Bolivia-Argentina), *nicotiana otophora*
Oxford 207 Hybrid, *nicotiana tabacum hybrid oxford 207*
Oxford 414NF Hybrid, *nicotiana tabacum hybrid oxford 414NF*
Oxford 6069 Hybrid, *nicotiana tabacum hybrid oxford 6069*
Oxford 940 Hybrid, *nicotiana tabacum hybrid oxford 940*
Paa (Argentina-Chile), *nicotiana paa*
Palmeri, *nicotiana palmeri*

Paniculata, *nicotiana paniculata*
Papante, *nicotiana rustica papante*
Paris Wrapper, *nicotiana tabacum paris wrapper*
Pauciflora (Chile), *nicotiana pauciflora*
Pavonii, *nicotiana rustica pavonii*
PD 312 LC Hybrid, *nicotiana tabacum hybrid pd 312 lc*
Pennbel 69 (type 41), *nicotiana tabacum pennbel 69 (type 41)*
Pennleaf-1, *nicotiana tabacum pennleaf-1*
Pennsylvania Broadleaf, *nicotiana tabacum pennsylvania broadleaf*
Pennsylvania Red, *nicotiana tabacum pennsylvania red*
Perfumed Antique lime, *nicotiana sanderae f1 permune antique lime*
Perfumed Blue, *nicotiana sanderae f1 perfumed blue*
Perfumed Bright Rose, *nicotiana sanderae f1 perfumed bright rose*
Perfumed Lime, *nicotiana sanderae f1 perfumed lime*
Perfumed Mixed, *nicotiana sanderae f1 perfumed mixed*
Perfumed Purple, *nicotiana sanderae f1 Deep purple*
Perfumed Red, *nicotiana sanderae f1 perfume red*
Perfumed White, *nicotiana sanderae f1 perfume white*
Perique, *nicotiana tabacum Perique*
Persian alata lime green, *nicotiana alata lime green*
Persian White, *nicotiana alata or affinis*
Petiolaris, *nicotiana petiolaris*
Petuniodes, *nicotiana petuniodes*
Pipeleaf Dark, *nicotiana tabacum pipeleaf dark*
Pretinho (Brazil), *nicotinan prentino*
Punche, *nicotiana rustica punche*
PVH 03 Hybrid, *nicotiana tabacum hybrid pvh 03*
PVH 08 Hybrid, *Nicotiana tabacum hybrid pvh 08*
PVH 09 Hybrid, *nicotiana tabacum hybrid pvh 09*
PVH 1118 Hybrid, *nicotiana tabacum hybrid pvh 1118*
PVH 1452 Hybrid, *nicotiana tabacum hybrid pvh 1452*
PVH 2110 Hybrid, *nicotiana tabacum hybrid ppvh 2110*
PVH 2275 Hybrid, *nicotiana tabacum hybrid pvh 2275*
Quadrivalvis, *nicotiana quadrivalvis*
Raimondii (Peru), *nicotiana raimondii*

Reams 158, *nicotiana tabacum reams 158*
Red Rose, *nicotiana tabacum red rose*
Red Russian, *nicotiana tabacum red russian*
RG 11 Hybrid, *nicotiana tabacum hybrid rg 11*
RG 17 Hybrid, *nicotiana tabacum hybrid rg 17*
RG 22 Hybrid, *nicotiana tabacum hybrid rg 22*
RG 4H217 Hybrid, *nicotiana tabacum hybrid rg 4h217*
RG 5H17 Hybrid, *nicotiana tabacum hybrid rg 5h17*
RG 7G13 Hybrid, *nicotiana tabacum hybrid rg 7g13*
RG 7G57 Hybrid, *nicotiana tabacum hybrid rg 7g57*
RG 7H13 Hybrid, *nicotiana tabacum hybrid rg 7h13*
RG 7H5 Hybrid, *nicotiana tabacum hybrid rg 7h5*
RG 81 Hybrid, *nicotiana tabacum hybrid rg 81*
RG H12 Hybrid, *nicotiana tabacum hybrid rg h12*
RG H4 Hybrid, *nicotiana tabacum hybrid rg h4*
RG H4 Hybrid, *nicotiana tabacum hybrid rg h4*
RG H51 Hybrid, *nicotiana tabacum hybrid rg h51*
RG H61 Hybrid, *nicotiana tabacum hybrid rg h61*
Rose, *nicotiana tabacum rosa*
Rosulata (Australia), *nicotiana rosulata*
Rotundifolia (Australia), *nicotiana rotundifolia*
Roulette Mixed, *nicotiana sanderae f2 roulette mixed*
Royal Velvet, *nicotiana tabacum royal velvet*
RS 1410 Hybrid, *nicotiana tabacum hybrid rs 1410*
Salta Blues, *nicotiana glauca*
Samsun-Canik (Turkey), *nicotiana tabacum canik*
Samsun-Maden (Turkey), *nicotiana tabacum maden*
San Juan Pueblo, *nicotiana rustica san juan pueblo*
Santo Domingo Ceremonial, *nicotiana rustica santo domingo ceremonial*
Saratoga Antique Shades, *nicotiana sanderae f1 saratoga antique shades*
Saratoga Appleblossom, *nicotiana sanderae f1 saratoga appleblossom*
Saratoga Deep Rose, *nicotiana sanderae f1 saratoga deep rose*
Saratoga Lime, *nicotiana sanderae f1 saratoga lime*

Saratoga Mixed, *nicotiana sanderae f1 saratoga mixed*
Saratoga pink, *nicotiana sanderae f1 Saratoga pink*
Saratoga Purple Bi-color, *nicotiana sanderae f1 saratoga purple bi-color*
Saratoga Red, *nicotiana sanderae f1 saratoga Red*
Saratoga Rose, *nicotiana sanderae f1 saratoga rose*
Saratoga White, *nicotiana sanderae f1 saratoga white*
Sears Special, *nicotiana tabacum sears special*
Sensation, *nicotiana sanderae f1 Sensation*
Setchellii, *nicotiana setchellii*
Shirazi (Iranian), *nicotiana tabacum shirazi*
Shirey, *nicotiana tabacum shirey*
Shrub, *nicotiana tomentosa*
Silk Leaf, *nicotiana tabacum silk leaf*
Simox, *nicotiana tabacum simox*
Simulans (Australia), *nicotiana simulans*
Sinop (Turkey), *nicotiana tabacum sinop*
Small Stalk Black Mammoth, *nicotiana tabacum small stalk black mammoth*
Solanifolia, *nicotiana solanifolia*
South American, *nicotiana sylvestris*
Southern, *nicotiana rustica Southern*
Southern Beauty, *nicotiana tabacum southern beauty*
Southern Tepehuan, *nicotiana rustica southern tepehuan*
Spagazzinii, *nicotiana spegazzinii*
Speight 102 Hybrid, *nicotiana tabacum hybrid speight 102*
Speight 168 Hybrid, *nicotiana tabacum hybrid speight 168*
Speight 168 Hybrid, *nicotiana tabacum hybrid speight 168*
Speight 172 Hybrid, *nicotiana tabacum hybrid speight 172*
Speight 178 Hybrid, *nicotiana tabacum hybrid speight 178*
Speight 179 Hybrid, *nicotiana tabacum hybrid speight 179*
Speight 190 Hybrid, *nicotiana tabacum hybrid speight 190*
Speight 196 Hybrid, *nicotiana tabacum hybrid speight 196*
Speight 206 Hybrid, *nicotiana tabacum hybrid speight 206*
Speight 208 Hybrid, *nicotiana tabacum hybrid speight 208*
Speight 209 Hybrid, *nicotiana tabacum nybrid speight 209*
Speight 210 Hybrid, *nicotiana tabacum hybrid speight 210*

Speight 211 Hybrid, *nicotiana tabacum hybrid speight 211*
Speight 212 Hybrid, *nicotiana tabacum hybrid speight 212*
Speight 220 Hybrid, *nicotiana tabacum hybrid speight 220*
Speight 225 Hybrid, *nicotiana tabacum hybrid speight 225*
Speight 227 Hybrid, *nicotiana tabacum hybrid speight 227*
Speight 234 Hybrid, *nicotiana tabacum hybrid speight 234*
Speight 235 Hybrid, *nicotiana tabacum hybrid speight 235*
Speight 236 Hybrid, *nicotiana tabacum hybrid speight 237*
Speight G-117 Hybrid, *nicotiana tabacum hybrid speight g-117*
Speight G-126 Hybrid, *Nicotiana tabacum hybrid speight g-126*
Speight G28 Hybrid, *nicotiana tabacum hybrid speight g-28*
Speight G-28 Hybrid, *nicotiana tabacum hybrid speight g-28*
Speight G70 Hybrid, *nicotiana tabacum hybrid speight g70*
Speight G-70 Hybrid, *nicotiana tabacum hybrid speight g-70*
Speight H20 Hybrid, *nicotiana tabacum hybrid speight h20*
Speight NF-3 Hybrid, *nicotiana tabacum hybrid speight nf-3*
Stag Horn, *nicotiana tabacum stag horn*
Starmaker Burgundy, *nicotiana sanderae f1 starmaker burgundy*
Starmaker Cherry Blossom, *nicotiana sanderae f1 starmaker cherry blossom*
Starmaker Lilac, *nicotiana sanderae f1 starmaker lilac*
Starmaker Mixed, *nicotiana sandera f1 starmaker mixed*
Starmaker Pink, *nicotiana sanderae f1 Starmaker Pink*
Starmaker Red, *nicotiana sanderae f1 starmaker red*
Starmaker Rose Pink, *nicotiana sanderae f1 starmaker rose pink*
Starmaker White, *nicotiana sanderae f1 starmaker white*
Starship Apple blossom, *nicotiana sanderae f1 starmaker appleblossom*
Stenocarpa, *nicotiana stenocarpa*
Stocktonii (Mexico), *nicotiana stocktonii*
Suaveleons, *nicotiana suaveleons*
Swarr Hibsman, *nicotiana tabacum swarr hibsman*
Sweet Scented, *nicotiana noctiflora*
Sylvestris, *nicotiana sylvestris*
Szamosi, *nicotiana tabacum szamosi*
Tanbaku (Persian), *nicotiana alata or affinis*
Tania Red Dwarf, *nicotiana sanderae f1 tania red dwarf*

Tarahumara El Cuervo, *nicotiana rustica tarahumara el cuervo*
Tasoua, *nicotiana tabacum tasoua*
Tasova (Turkey), *nicotiana tabacum tasova*
Tekne (Hungarian), *nicotiana tabacum tekne*
Tennessee Red, *nicotiana tabacum tennessee red*
Texana, *nicotiana rustica texana*
Tex-Mex, *nicotiana plumbagubufolia*
Thrysiflora, *nicotiana thrysiflora*
Thuoc Lao, *nicotiana rustica thuoc lao*
Tinkerbell, *nicotiana sanderae f2 tinkerbell*
TN D94 Hybrid, *nicotiana tabacum hybrid tn d94*
TND 950 LC Hybrid, *nicotiana tabacum hybrid tnd 950 lc*
Tomentosa, *nicotiana tomentosa*
Tomentosiformis (Bolivia), *nicotiana tomentosiformis*
Tonaquillo, *nicotiana obtusifolia*
Trabzon (Turkey), *nicotiana tabacum trabzon*
Tree (USA-SW), *nicotiana glauca*
Truncata (Australia), *nicotiana truncata*
Tutakano, *nicotiana rustica tutakano*
Umbratica (Australia), *nicotiana umbratica*
Undulata (Chile), *nicotiana undulata*
VA 116 Hybrid, *nicotiana tabacum hybrid va 116*
VA 119, *nicotiana tabacum va 119*
VA 359, *nicotiana tabacum va 359*
VA 359, *nicotiana tabacum va 359*
VA 407, *nicotiana tabacum va 407*
VA 409, *nicotiana tabacum va409*
VA116, *nicotiana tabacum va 116*
VA312, *nicotiana tabacum va312*
VA355, *nicotiana tabacum va355*
Velutina (Australia), *nicotiana velutina*
Vesta 64, *nicotiana tabacum vesta 64*
VH Madole, *nicotiana tabacum vh madole*
Virginia, *nicotiana tabacum virginia*
Virginia 310, *nicotiana tabacum virginia 310*